COLLINGWOOD AND BRITISH ID
VOLUME 7

CW00504058

COLLINGWOOD AND BRITISH IDEALISM STUDIES

Volume Seven
2000

Identities and Differences

Edited by
DAVID BOUCHER
BRUCE HADDOCK
ANDREW VINCENT

Society

Published by the R. G. Collingwood Society
Registered Charity No. 1037636
School of European Studies
Cardiff University, P.O. Box 908
Cardiff CF10 3YQ

http://www.cf.ac.uk/euros/collingwood/collingwood.html

ISSN 1356-0670
ISBN 0 9524393 7 9

British Library Cataloguing in Publication Data.
A catalogue record of this book is available from the British Library.

© World Copyright: Collingwood Society, 2000

*No part of any contribution may be reproduced in any form
without permission, except for the quotation of brief passages
in criticism and discussion.*

Printed in Wales, UK, by Dinefwr Press, Llandybïe

THE R. G. COLLINGWOOD SOCIETY

Officers of the Society

HON. PRESIDENTS   TERESA COLLINGWOOD SMITH
VERA COLLINGWOOD (Deceased)

TRUSTEES   DAVID BOUCHER (Chairman)
BRUCE HADDOCK
JAMES CONNELLY

ADMINISTRATOR   SUZIE WILLIAMS

EDITORS OF *COLLINGWOOD*   DAVID BOUCHER
AND BRITISH IDEALISM   BRUCE HADDOCK
STUDIES   ANDREW VINCENT

EDITORIAL BOARD

Professor Rex Martin (Kansas); Professor Lionel Rubinoff (Trent University, Canada); Professor H. S. Harris (York University, Canada); Professor W. Jan van der Dussen (Open University, Netherlands); Professor Leon Pompa (Birmingham); Professor Leon J. Goldstein (State University of New York at Binghampton); Professor W. H. Dray (University of Ottawa, Canada); Professor Luciano Dondoli (Cassino, Italy); Professor Mikail Kissel (Russian Academy of Sciences, Moscow); Peter Nicholson (York); Ian Hodder (Cambridge) Terry Diffey (Sussex); James Connelly (Southampton Institute); Heikki Saari (Helsinki); Professor James Patrick (St. Thomas More, U.S.A.); Professor Alasdair MacIntyre (Notre Dame, U.S.A.); Professor Michael Krausz (Bryn Mawr, U.S.A.); Professor Donald Taylor (Oregon, U.S.A.); Professor Guido Vanheeswijck (Antwerp and Louvain); Rik Peters (Groningen).

COLLINGWOOD & BRITISH IDEALISM CENTRE:

Presidents: Lord Raymond Plant and Teresa Collingwood Smith.
Professorial Fellows: Rex Martin, David Boucher, Andrew Vincent.
Senior Fellows: Bruce Haddock, Peter Nicholson, James Connelly.

REGISTERED CHARITY NO. 1037636

School of European Studies
Cardiff University, P.O. Box 980, Cardiff, CF10 3YO

TABLE OF CONTENTS

Editors' Introduction ⸻ viii

JAMES PATRICK   Eliot and the New Idealism:
Poetry and History at Oxford
1914-1915 ⸻ 1

DONALD TAYLOR   Collingwood's Developing Aesthetic:
Artists and Audiences ⸻ 32

GIUSEPPINA D'ORO   On Collingwood's Conceptions
of History ⸻ 45

Collingwood Corner

JAMES CONNELLY   Collingwood and His Contemporaries:
responses to critics 1918-1928
(with illustrations)
compiled by James Connelly ⸻ 72

SUSAN DANIEL   R. G. Collingwood: Recent Publications   94

British Idealism

MARIA DIMOVA-
COOKSON   T. H. Green and Justifying Human
Rights ⸻ 97

COLIN TYLER   'THIS DANGEROUS DRUG OF VIOLENCE':
Making Sense of Bernard Bosanquet's
Theory of Punishment ⸻ 116

Review

David Boucher, James Connelly and Tariq Modood (eds.),
*Philosophy, History and Civilization: Interdisciplinary Perspectives
on R. G. Collingwood.* Cardiff: University of Wales Press, 1995.
xviii + 388 pp. ISBN 0-7083-1308-6 (hbk).
By Stamatoula Panagakou ⸻ 141

List of Life Members ⸻ 148

Introduction

In consultation with Teresa Smith and the Trustees of the Collingwood Society the journal has changed its title to reflect what always was the broader remit of the Collingwood Centre at Swansea. The Centre has now moved to the School of European Studies, Cardiff University where its resources have been broadened and increased. Sue Irving administered the Centre with admirable efficiency and was one of our finest assets. Unfortunately she was not able to move to Cardiff with the Centre. As the public face of the Collingwood Society and Centre she has been greatly missed by our many members. We are fortunate, however, in now being able to call upon the services of Suzi Williams who has already contributed a great deal to our continuing activities. Academics associated with the Centre at Swansea, continue their commitment to its aims and remain professorial and senior fellows along with the additions of Peter Nicholson, and Lord Plant who, with Teresa Smith, is President of the Collingwood and British Idealism Centre.

The Collingwood Centre has become the Collingwood and British Idealism Centre, and holds, in addition to many Ph.D.s and manuscripts relating to Collingwood, copies of manuscripts relating to Henry Jones, Michael Oakeshott, and the Australian Idealists William Mitchell and Francis Anderson. Our aim is to broaden the interest base in our activities and to secure the long-term future of the journal *Collingwood and British Idealism Studies*. The Centre has already staged two very successful conferences at Aberdare Hall in Cardiff, and Gregynog near Newtown, Montgomeryshire on aspects of the thought of Collingwood and the British Idealists, and between 4-6 July, 2001 will continue its commitment to promote the life and thought of Collingwood in staging another of our three day conferences St Catherine's College, Oxford. Two of the editors of the journal have collaborated on the first major book to emerge from the new Centre, *British Idealism and Political Theory*, which was published by Edinburgh University Press in November of 2000.

The Collingwood Society, a charitable trust, remains the keystone in the arch of all our activities and is responsible for publishing the journal and ensuring that the aims of the organisation are upheld.

David Boucher
Bruce Haddock
Andrew Vincent

Eliot and the New Idealism: Poetry and History at Oxford, 1914-1915

JAMES PATRICK
The College of Saint Thomas More

What we admire in genuine works of art is the perfect imaginative form that a state of mind assumes there.
Benedetto Croce, *Guide to Aesthetics*[1]

The goal seems to me to be essentially the same as with Aquinas and Dante . . ., the development and subsumption of emotion and feeling through intellect . . .
T. S. Eliot, *Clark Lectures*[2]

The poet converts human experience into poetry . . . by fusing thought into emotion. Thus Dante has fused the Thomistic philosophy into a poem expressing what it feels like to be a Thomist.
R. G. Collingwood, *Principles of Art*[3]

The influence of F. H. Bradley on Eliot's poetry and criticism has been much canvassed, but Eliot's debt to that other idealism current in the university in the first autumn of the Great War, the idealism of Benedetto Croce that John Alexander Smith and R. G. Collingwood advocated in lectures, informals, and common rooms, has not been much studied.[4] True, philosophic commonalities shared by T. S. Eliot and R. G. Collingwood were noticed early by Alan Donagan, who suggested that Eliot's essays had influenced Collingwood; by Eric Thompson, who investigated certain shared metaphysical themes; and more recently by Guido Vanheeswijck, who explored the common dependence of Eliot and Collingwood on the romantic tradition, but the influence of Croce on Eliot by way of his Oxford teachers remains largely unexplored.[5]

This said, codicils are in order. Essays on influences suggest and illuminate, but they are rarely if ever conclusive, capable of demonstrating the passage of thought from text to text or mind to mind. This is especially true when the field of inquiry contains, as it does in the case of twentieth century English idealism, many similar themes emanating from mutually sympathetic sources. Freed, who believed Eliot was heavily dependant on Bradley, expressed his frustration by claiming that 'though Bradley is Eliot's man, he is not always the best expositor of Eliot; on some points Joachim is more helpful, or Bosanquet, or Nettleship, or A. E. Taylor – and I have found that Brand Blanshard throws a retrospective light on certain aspects of Bradley's philosophy.'[6] In claiming that Croce influenced Eliot at one important moment no inference that the influence of Bradley or Royce or Bosanquet was absent is intended. But in fact Eliot's Oxford year was an intense encounter with one variety of idealism, the Crocean idealism that would engage the minds of his teachers during the years after 1909.

The philosophers to whose instruction Eliot was directed by his Merton tutor Harold Joachim, himself an idealist and Smith's philosophic ally, were the stalwarts of the movement called in 1914, or soon to be called, the New Idealism. Now largely neglected as an intellectual dead end, the title, given on an analogy with the New Realism of H. A. Prichard and the Harvard Six, the New Psychology of John Watson, the New Criticism of John Crow Ransom and Donald Davidson, and the New Theology of R. J. Campbell, appears evanescently in monographs and books in the period 1918-1932. Its principals were Joachim and John Alexander Smith, its acolytes H. Wildon Carr and Alfred Hoernle, and its promising disciples Robin George Collingwood, H. J. Paton, and G. R. G. Mure.[7] Its sources were Aristotle and Plato, English Hegelianism, Kant, the school of Thomas Hill Green, and, notoriously, the Italian idealists Benedetto Croce and Giovanni Gentile.

Smith, already famous as an Aristotelian scholar, had surprised Oxford in 1909 by casting his inaugural to the Waynflete Professorship of Moral and Metaphysical Philosophy as an extended exposition of Croce's philosophy and by referring thereafter to Croce as his master. Although Joachim shared Smith's interest in Aristotle more than his enthusiasm for Croce, the deference Joachim accorded Smith, who had campaigned effectively for Joachim's election to the Wykeham professorship in 1919, was famous; Eliot, after a month in the University knew that Joachim and Smith were hand in glove.[8] Smith's sponsorship of Collingwood may be traced at least from 1912, when Collingwood, newly elected to a Pembroke fellowship, dined with Smith at Balliol, Magdalen, and at the Aristotelian Society dinner; through Collingwood's translation of Croce's *Philosophy of Giambattista Vico* in 1913, which Smith duly praised; to Collingwood's translation of Croce's *Autobiography* (for which Smith wrote the preface); and finally to Smith's reflection at the time of his retirement from the Waynflete chair – to which he recommended Collingwood – that Collingwood had done much of his thinking for him.[9] When Eliot met Collingwood in October 1914, Collingwood was deep in the Italians. In 1912 he had read Croce's *Logica*; in the spring and summer of 1913 Collingwood had completed his translation of Croce's *Vico*, receiving Croce's corrections on October 27; and between December 16 and 20, 1913, Collingwood read the *Esthetica*. The maturity of the Collingwood-Smith friendship was marked by Collingwood's faithful attendance at Smith's lectures, and occasions, noted in Collingwood's diary, professors might reserve for chosen disciples like dinner in Soho before *Figaro* at the Drury Lane.[10] Certainly Collingwood would have been of the party when Smith entertained Croce at Magdalen College in 1923. To study with Smith and Collingwood in 1914-1915 was to swim in a Crocean stream.

The New Idealism rarely finds place in accounts of the post-Great War period, partly because its history was written by the realists, victors in the philosophic wars of the twenties, who considered idealism in any form wrongheaded and ephemeral; partly because J. A. Smith, its public defender in the University, controversial during his professorial tenure from 1909 to 1935, was easily discredited retrospectively by the newly unfashionable assertiveness of his broad and allusive scholarly style, replete with Hegel-like references to Spirit, History, and the Real, a style which, when assessed against the background of neatly tentative and implicitly skeptical conclusions framed in the realists' diffident prose, seemed pompous and naive.

A polymath who thought the Teutonic ideal of the expert an academic curse, Smith was disliked by Bertrand Russell, considered an embarrassment by Lord Cherwell and a genial fraud by Paul Elmer Moore (who nonetheless appreciated his hospitality), but H. H. Joachim, the finest philosophic mind in the pre-war school, held Smith in something like awe and Collingwood in his *Autobiography* named Smith and Joachim the best philosophers of the Great War period. C. S. Lewis wrote that living in the same stairwell with Professor Smith was itself a liberal education, and Royce thought Smith 'as dialectical as Mephistopheles, – although otherwise a beautiful person.'[11]

That the place of Eliot's Oxford year in his intellectual development has come into scholarly focus slowly has perhaps been inspired partly by Eliot's subsequent abandonment of philosophy and his attendant silence about his philosophic studies. When Eliot praised Bradley, the foil for his unpublished doctoral dissertation, it was not for his philosophy but for his style, and when Joachim died in August 1938, he was remembered in the *Times* by Eliot not for teaching him idealism but for teaching him what he wanted to say and how to say it. Following Eliot's lead, his intellectual biographers have usually ignored his Oxford year. Eric Thompson, whose book was an early essay in Eliot's intellectual biography, was either unaware that Eliot had undertaken formal study in Merton College in 1914-1915 or convinced that this year had no importance for Eliot's intellectual biography, and more recent studies fail to mention Croce, Smith or Collingwood as sources or influences.[12] These omissions may be explained in part by the fact that Eliot's letters of the Great War period, in which he catalogued his Oxford studies and wrote candidly of his growing disenchantment with philosophy, were not published until 1988, nor the Clark Lectures, given at Cambridge in 1926, which display an aesthetic of language that presupposes Croce's thought, until 1993. But the letters, the Cambridge lectures, and Eliot's early criticism, especially 'Tradition and the Individual Talent' (1917), suggest that his Oxford year had not left Eliot uninfluenced, that Croce, for knowledge of whom Smith and Collingwood were obvious sources, had a significant if unacknowledged part in the making of Eliot's mind during his Oxford year. Of course, in the autumn of 1914 the imminent collapse of idealism was foreseen no more clearly than the impending political failure of Europe. Joachim was the author of a much praised book, *The Nature of Truth* (1906) and Smith, who that year narrowly missed election to the mastership of Balliol, was the acknowledged head of a lively philosophic school that included not only Joachim but Clement Webb and Hastings Rashdall.[13] Eliot, probably mistaking the influence of Croce for that of Hegel – Smith had not read Hegel systematically,[14] – did write that Smith was the first and only old-fashioned Hegelian he had met, and noted as well the difficulties in 'getting anywhere' with Joachim in general philosophical discussion because of Joachim's Hegelianism and Eliot's own 'fatal disposition toward skepticism,' but Eliot's judgment, echoing Collingwood's own, was that Joachim was the best lecturer in the wartime University and that Smith and Joachim were 'undoubtedly the two best men in Oxford.'[15]

I

When Eliot arrived at Merton in October 1914 his mind was already marked by convictions that would be developed over a lifetime. At Harvard Eliot had been deeply influenced by Irving Babitt, humanist and anti-romantic, who had taught Eliot a deep suspicion of democracy and directed him to French political intellectuals associated with *Action Francaise*, Charles Maurras and Georges Sorel; to the critic Remy de Gourmont; and to T. E. Hulme, the English proponent of humanism and classicism. If by 1914 he had not met Hulme, whom he called in his Cambridge lectures of 1926 'the most *fertile* mind of my generation and one of the glories of this University,' Eliot had certainly been educated in Hulme's anti-romanticism by Babbit.[16] Through Babitt and Hulme Eliot was already familiar with the critical stance that included rejection of the romantic ideas that poetry is an expression of the poet's personality or feelings or an affective recommendation of morality.[17]

Eliot knew Bertrand Russell before he came to Oxford because he had attended Russell's lectures at Harvard in 1913, and although Eliot and Russell were to become great friends, in Eliot's mature judgement Russell's philosophy was not only destructive but self-destructive. Chapters IV and V of Eliot's Harvard dissertation are a sustained attack on Russell's realist epistemology, and he later wrote that he could never make sense of Russell's little symbols.[18]

By 1914 Eliot was well versed in the idealist tradition through his Harvard professor Josiah Royce and during his last fall semester Eliot had learned something of contemporary English Idealism from the metaphysics course taught by Alfred Hoernlé, whom Royce had brought into the Harvard faculty when he could not lure J. A. Smith away from Oxford or cause Bertrand Russell, who had visited in 1913, to stay.[19] And in the fall of 1914 Eliot was familiar with the greatest of the Oxford idealists, F. H. Bradley, as only a dissertation writer can be with his subject. but even Bradley's authority was not accepted uncritically. Dissertations, Eliot wrote during his Oxford year, ought to be written by those who no longer accepted the ideas they were defending. and when he began to rewrite his dissertation in 1915, Eliot noted that his revision would be 'entirely destructive' of Bradley's theory of judgement on behalf of his own thesis that it is 'simply a waste of time to define judgement at all.'[20] Yet if Eliot was in 1915 too skeptical to be passionately partisan in the realist-idealist wars, he was nonetheless drawn in his tentative Eliotic way to the idealist camp, unwilling to abandon the idealist principles of the internality of relations and degrees of reality and leery of the obvious alternative, G. E. Moore and his disciples.[21] Eliot thought his Merton tutor 'the best philosopher here,' while the realist paladin H. A. Prichard was merely 'good.'[22] The classicism of Babbit, a certain sympathy for idealism, if only on the grounds that it made a quasi-rational skepticism possible, and an unwillingness to become a disciple of Russell's positivism were already characteristic. If it was not yet easy to foresee the Eliot of 1927 – 'I am a classicist, a royalist, and an Anglo-Catholic' – it was possible to discern in 1914 a suspicion of democracy and positivism, a love of hierarchy and an unwillingness, deeper than his philosophical skepticism, to imagine a meaningless world.

During the three terms of the academic year 1914-15 Eliot faithfully wrote his Harvard advisor James Houghton Wood describing the course of his studies at Oxford. Just before his arrival (5 October 1914), Eliot had been plugging away at Husserl and 'going through the *Metaphysics* for the first time in Greek.' That Michaelmas term of 1914 Eliot 'followed three courses of lectures, Joachim on the *Ethics*, Collingwood's (of Pembroke) on the *De Anima*, and J. A. Smith's logic.'[23] Collingwood's text and notes for his *De Anima* lectures may be found, bound by the author with

Ruskinian attention to the consonance of beauty and utility, in the Bodleian; Eliot's text with its marginal notations is in the Heywood Collection at King's College, Cambridge. During the term Eliot promised to send Woods his notes on Collingwood's lectures.[24] Colllingwood's first impression of the slight American who signed himself T. Stearns Eliot and whom Joachim had directed to his *De Anima* lectures is not known, but Eliot wrote Wood on November 9: 'Collingwood is a young person, but very good, I think.'

When Hilary term began Eliot reported: 'I am continuing with Joachim's and Smith's lectures and with Joachim's *Posterior Analytics* and am taking a class in Plotinus with Stewart. I shall go to Smith's and I expect Stewart's informals as well. For Joachim I am writing a paper on Plato, and I shall later write on Aristotle.' In Trinity term Eliot read the *Ethics* with Joachim, attended 'some lectures by J. A. Smith on the concept of value' and a short course by McDougall.[25]

With Joachim as his tutor Eliot had gained access to formidable talents in the explication of the text of Aristotle and Plato. Smith, despite his enthusiasm for the Italians after his election to the Waynflete Professorship in 1909, had made his reputation as an Aristotelian scholar. Elected president of the Oxford Aristotelian Society in succession to Ingram Bywater in 1907, after 1910 Smith was editor with W. D. Ross of the *Oxford Aristotle*, although Smith was himself able to translate only the *De Anima* and was finally dropped or resigned, probably because he found finishing anything too difficult. He was a compelling teacher who offered semester by semester, often with Joachim, a seminar on an Aristotelian text, and who in his sixty-fifth year decided to undertake a new translation of the *Organon* because he had previously been too much influenced by other translations.[26] Professor Burnet, recommending Smith to the Waynflete chair, wrote: 'I know very few men who combine as happily a rare width of intellectual interest with complete mastery of such pictures of the field as he has had to do with more immediately. Mr. Smith is deeply imbued with the best traditions of Oxford Aristotelianism.'[27] Even A. J. Ayer, who considered Smith's idealism great nonsense, also thought him 'a good comparative philologist and well schooled in the texts of Aristotle.'[28] Joachim's Aristotle seminar was famous, and it was for his reading of the *Posterior Analytics* that Eliot thanked Joachim in the *Times* in 1938.

By directing Eliot to Smith and Collingwood, Joachim made Eliot at least for his Oxford year, a disciple of the Smith-Collingwood connection, locating his American student in an intellectual milieu in which the dominant living philosopher was Benedetto Croce. In his 1936 lectures on the philosophy of history, later included by T. M. Knox in *The Idea of History*,[29] Collingwood, perhaps the best witness to the content of the Crocean themes important in scholarly conversation in 1914, catalogued the development of Croce's thought from the 1893 essay 'History Subsumed under the Concept of Art' through the publication in 1912 and 1913 of the essay that formed the heart of *Teoria e Storia della Storiographia*. The themes of Croce's philosophy as Collingwood recalled them in 1936 were:

1) Croce's insistence, advanced in the essay 'History Subsumed under the Concept of Art' in 1893 and later in the *Aesthetic* (1902) that poetry, indeed all art, is engaged through particular and individual representation, a point Collingwood took over whole and one Eliot, who disliked the abstraction to which philosophers were given, reiterated;

2) the theory presented in Croce's *Logic* in 1909 that the individual, without losing its individuality, attains significance by representing the universal, which Eliot would call the concrete universal;

3) the idea advanced in essays of 1912 and 1913 that history is always contemporary, the complex activity of living imagination that incorporates the past as it changes the past, an idea central to Collingwood's *Idea of History* and to Eliot's 1919 essay 'Tradition and the Individual Talent'; and

4) Croce's assertion in the same essays of the unity of thought and feeling, intellect and emotion in poetry, a unity related to 2) above, that made poetry the means through which thought acquired the body of feeling and feeling the intelligibility of thought. This idea, coupled with the idea that history could be understood only by entering into the mind of its subjects, led in one way to Collingwood's controversial theory of reenactment and in another to Eliot's conviction that poetry made it possible to enter into realms of thought with a subjectivity so complete that one could feel the metaphysics of Donne or St. Thomas. These ideas close

upon themselves in the idea that poetry was successful when it represented sensibility with integrity and provided background for the failure to do so which Eliot called dissociation of sensibility and Collingwood corruption of consciousness. This failure is what Croce was describing when he wrote: 'Do you wish to understand the true history of a Neolithic Ligurian or Sicilian? Try, if you can, to become a Neolithic Ligurian or Sicilian in your mind. If you cannot do that, or do not care to, content yourself with describing and arranging in series the skulls, implements, and drawings which have been found belonging to these Neolithic peoples.'[30]

These idealist ideas were familiar perhaps in part because Eliot had after all read Bradley – he had bought *Appearance and Reality* in June 1913 – and had been taught by Royce at Harvard.[31] But the Crocean emphasis upon history as the form of experience was not central to Bradleian idealism and Croce's insistence that art makes thought into feeling should not be confused with the general Bradleian and Hegelian notion that the ideal always becomes incarnate in history. Nevertheless Eliot thought within the idealist tradition, in part because the Oxford idealists were also often Aristotelians, respectful of the broad tradition of classical philosophic thought, and because Eliot and Collingwood, who were contemporaries – Collingwood was one year Eliot's junior – were sympathetic to the synthetic philosophic tradition that idealism encouraged and were, Eliot gently, Collingwood stridently, critics of the Prichard-Russell-Moore philosophy with its insistence that philosophy began with Hume. Collingwood explained his rejection of realism and his interest in the great tradition to the Pembroke philosophy club in 1923, an explanation then recorded in the minutes only by title, but given in passionate detail in his *Autobiography* in 1939: the realists had in ethics attacked the moral philosophy of the School of Green and had replaced it with contempt for philosophy, and on the ever-vexed epistemological question had taught that knowledge changed neither knower nor known.[32]

After 1918 the paths taken by Collingwood and his soon to be famous pupil diverged. Collingwood, having been born to the embattled philosophic tradition of Ruskin and Green – his father was Ruskin's last secretary – and reared at Lanehead, his father's house at the end of the lane leading to

Ruskin's Brantwood, persisted in the defense of that tradition even as he suffered from the loneliness his allegiance caused. Eliot, to the disappointment of his Harvard professors (and his mother), abandoned philosophy, chiefly because he had discovered that poetry was his metier. In July following his Oxford year Eliot wrote, 'I see a possibility of being able to express myself through literary channels; and this I prefer to the makeshift of professional philosophy . . . I felt that the work at Harvard was deadening me. And the prospect of becoming a professor at some provincial university in America is not stimulating.'[33] This self-dramatization belied the fact that Harvard, convincingly provincial only from the vantage point of Oxford, was anxious to continue his travelling fellowship or to appoint Eliot an assistant in its philosophy faculty. But Eliot had by the end of the year turned his back on philosophy, never taking time to stand his viva for his Harvard degree, and although he would, beginning in the mid-twenties, take up the Catholic Revival, its historiography and its native metaphysic, quite unapologetically, Eliot remained sphinx-like regarding any philosophical debts he may have incurred earlier. In the twenties and thirties the poet was often patronizing toward philosophy and philosophers. The tone of his criticism of Coleridge was typical: the philosopher had lacked intellectual rigor; 'Coleridge's metaphysical interest was quite genuine, and was like most metaphysical interest an affair of the emotions. But a literary critic should have no emotions except those provoked by a work of art, and these (as I have already hinted) are, when valid, probably not emotions at all.'[34] And philosophers had, Eliot believed, been implicated in the destruction of the definiteness of language: 'No one who had not witnessed the event could imagine the conviction in the voice of Professor Eucken as he pounded the table and exclaimed, 'Was ist geist? Geist ist . . .'[35]

Eliot's disappointment with philosophy was generated by his skepticism, and his skepticism was grounded in a fine sense of the limitations of philosophy, which invariably met 'with partial failure – and with partial success.'[36] In the winter of his Oxford year (November 27) Eliot voiced the decidedly anti-classical conclusion: 'I have had for several years a distrust of strong convictions in any theory or creed which can be formulated.' Relativism had its lessons: 'not to pursue anything to a conclusion and to avoid complete consistency.' Real knowledge could be gained from science, a world 'unsatisfying , but the most satisfactory we know,' or from art, but philosophy was a texture of unprovable ideas that collapsed when forced into the real world.[37]

Later Eliot would say that his disappointment with philosophy had probably sprung from the inability of the philosophy he knew to find its completion in theology,[38] and indeed theology became, as Eliot's thought matured in the twenties, the necessary capstone of the intellectual enterprise, revelation neatly rescuing philosophy from relativism. This idealism, a philosophy which with studied ambiguity naturalized the concept spirit, inverted the classical relation between theology and philosophy, and routinely subordinated revelation to philosophy, collapsing the City of God into the historical process, was unable to do. Eliot's anti-liberal sentiments, his classicism, had always driven him toward the ideal of an ordered intellect in an ordered society. Eliot's interest during the years 1914-1925 in Charles Maurras, an atheist who nevertheless considered the certain authority of Catholicism the political salvation of France, may have encouraged Eliot to the view that neither society nor knowledge could be saved from a debilitating relativism apart from an appeal to some extra-philosophic source, an insight that would encourage Eliot's conversion from a highly philosophic and abstract Unitarianism to a history laden, sacramental Anglo-Catholicism in 1927. It was only as Eliot during the twenties took up the writers of the French Catholic Revival, Etienne Gilson and Jacques Maritain, but also Cardinal Mercier, Martin D'Arcy, and Maurice DeWulf, that Eliot appropriated the idea of an organic, non-authoritarian relation between philosophy and theology, nature and grace, within which philosophy was propaedeutic to theology and theology perfective of reason along those frontiers at which philosophy must fall silent.[39] Eliot summarized this position in 1952: 'By affirming the dependence of philosophy upon revelation and a proper respect for the wisdom of the ancients, he [Pieper] puts the philosopher himself in proper relation to other philosophers living and dead.'[40] But in 1914-1915 the Oxford philosophy Eliot knew, neither Bradley nor the idealism of the Smith-Collingwood connection, afforded a way out of skepticism. Idealism could only represent theology as philosophy misunderstood. When in 1916 he reviewed in the *International Journal of Ethics* both William Temple's *Mens Creatrix* and Collingwood's *Religion and Philosophy*, although Eliot spoke politely of his Oxford teacher, he criticized both authors for their reduction of Christian theology, which by 1916 Eliot clearly saw depended, if it were anything at all, upon certain historical facts that could not be reduced to ideas, to a kind of faux philosophy.[41]

To understand the history of Eliot's philosophic commitments is to begin with the fact that beneath his tendency to deny all influences by silence and all affirmations by a careful texture of qualifications, Eliot's philosophy developed through two periods. After 1926 – and here the Clark Lectures themselves are the principal evidence – Eliot assumed in a general way the force of the neoscholastic view that the mind could know truth and that philosophy was perfected by theology, its invariably relativistic character shored up as it were by revelation. Of this position his essay prefatory to Josef Pieper's *Leisure the Basis of Culture* is the best evidence.

Eliot's philosophic commitments before the mid-twenties lie in shadows he created. He praised Bradley's prose style, but wrote his dissertation to destroy Bradley's theory of judgement. Eliot thanked his Oxford tutor for teaching him to say what he wanted to say but not for anything that could be called Joachim's philosophy. A friend of Russell, Eliot was no particular friend of Russell's philosophy. Eliot's silence on Collingwood and Croce was part of his silence regarding that philosophical past of the years before 1925. Eliot had certainly met Croce. Eliot noted in 1920 that while on a bicycle trip up the Loire he stopped in Paris and dined twice with Fritz Vanderpyl, Croce, and James Joyce.[42] Eliot kept up his acquaintance with Collingwood, inviting him to become a reviewer for the *Criterion*.[43] It was not surprising that when the *Principles of Art* was published Eliot called it 'that very remarkable book.' He could hardly do less since the illustration upon which Collingwood's argument turned was *The Waste Land*, Eliot, having been presented in the concluding pages of *Principles of Art* as the 'one great poet.'[44] And for Collingwood, Eliot was that prize of teaching, a successful, famous, former student.

Despite his reticence, the voice of Crocean idealism, unmistakable if unacknowledged, represented in 1914-1915 by Smith and Collingwood, may be discerned, conglomerate with other ideas acquired and original, in the contrapuntal staff of Eliot's criticism from the beginning. It was, one reviewer noticed in 1936, more likely that Eliot had learned that thought and feeling were fused in poetry from Signore Croce than from

I. A. Richards,[45] and he might have added that the idea that thought is a living, summary tradition, was arguably a gift of his Oxford year and hence of Crocean idealism. The mediating theme was history, which Eliot saw his teachers using in a distinctively Oxfordian way. History, Eliot wrote, was an aristocratic discipline, characteristic of Oxford, while Cambridge was the home of natural science, and it was, Eliot wrote to Professor Woods (9 November 1914), 'especially the historical side' of Oxford philosophy that evoked his 'keen admiration.' A few months later, having concluded that he did not wish to spend another year at Oxford, he added (2 March) that he would want to go where he could continue his work on Greek philosophy, 'and perhaps on other periods in the history of philosophy,' for 'the historical and critical aspect is that which now appeals to me the most strongly.'[46] The Oxford idealists' philosophy had encouraged a way of imagining the past for which his teachers would have provided the example. Smith and Collingwood philosophized synoptically, Aristotle and the Italian idealists appearing as coordinate and complementary authorities in a great tradition that Smith called Mind and Eliot the European mind.

II

'Tradition and the Individual Talent,' published in the *Egoist* in December 1919, was an essay on the relation between past and present and between contemporary poets and the great literary tradition. The essay came at the moment when European civilization was rejecting its own past, digging a moat across memory that marked a sharp division between a world of war, death, and empires, and a brave new world of women's suffrage, Marxist revolution, and automobiles. The past existed to be overcome, and the project of overcoming it was at least superficially successful. C. S. Lewis, who returned to Oxford from the war in January 1919, later wrote that there was more distance between the world of the thirties and Jane Austen than between Austen and Plato; and Virginia Woolf believed that the post-impressionist exhibit of 1910 marked the invention of a new human nature.'[47]

In the context of Europe's flight from its past Eliot's was a masterful exposition of an idea rooted ultimately in Hegel and implicitly in the idealism of Royce and Bradley, and developed by Croce and the Smith-Collingwood school at Oxford as the key to their understanding of history. The past, to the degree that it is available to memory through texts and artifacts, is always present and the present is our consciousness of the past.[48] The author of 'The Theory of History,' a typescript of 1914 in the Smith Papers in the Magdalen College archives, spoke for the school when he wrote that all history is 'ideally contemporary.'[49] J. A. Smith's 1915 essay 'The Contribution of Greece and Rome' began: 'It might appear a paradox to preface a discourse on the ancient world by asserting that the only genuine and important history is con-temporary history. Yet reflection on this doctrine will show that it is not only consistent with a serious and steady interest in what is called antiquity (and indeed the past in general), but its only rational basis and justification.'[50] Antiquarianism, Smith wrote in an essay on ancient philosophy, 'is fatal to philosophy, as it is also the deepest foe of history. The true reason for the study of the ancients is that their problems are still our problems, their selves our selves. Their world is ours also, and all this they present to us with a youthful freshness and vividness.'[51] Classical antiquity 'is not a dead world; its deeds and thoughts are not past but still live, still 'breathe and burn' in us. They are largely the stuff of which our present selves and present world are made. We *are* the Greeks and Romans, made what we now are by their deeds and thoughts and experiences . . .'[52]

The position of the Croceans was not the absolutism of Bradley and Bosanquet, in which willing minds might discern at least the passing shadow of the Christian God. For the Croceans, the internal relations discerned by self-consciousness were not located within the Absolute but were firmly rooted in self-consciousness, in the person, who, moment by moment, lived the life of the Spirit. Croce's philosophy, hence Smith's, professed 'no more than to illuminate the present,' disclaiming 'all doctrines concerning primordial origins and ultimate ends, eschewing all archaeologies and transcendentalisms and eschatologies, and concentrating itself upon the interpretation of that history which the spirit of Man incessantly enacts and creates.'[53] While this use of Spirit represented little progress toward defining and exorcizing the ghost that had inhabited the philosophical closet of Western thought since Hegel, the Crocean insistence that time was real made history the dominant category. The Real, Smith wrote, 'is a (or the) History, and every genuine part of it is historical . . . I am therefore obliged to reject the counter-doctrine that the Absolute, while containing all histories, is and has no history, and so at the outset of my philosophizing to part company with Bradley . . .'.[54] The life of mankind, reflective life, was then the creation of the self through self-knowledge, knowledge being always historical. Almost nothing in Collingwood's idea of history may not be found, in fusty, mellifluous form, in Smith's essays and lectures. When Collingwood wrote: 'The historical process is a process in which man creates for himself this or that kind of human nature by recreating in his own thought the past to which he is heir,' he was identifying experience and tradition, or history.[55]

So was Eliot when, in 'Tradition and the Individual Talent,' he effected the transposition of the philosophic idea to literature. 'Tradition involves the historical sense, which we may call nearly indispensable to anyone who would continue to be a poet beyond his twenty-fifth year; and the historical sense involves a perception, not only of the pastness of the past, but of its presence; the historical compels a man to write not merely with his own generation in his bones, but with a feeling that the whole literature of Europe from Homer and within the whole of the literature of his own country has a simultaneous existence and composes a simultaneous order. This historical sense, which is a sense of the timeless as well as the temporal and of the timeless and temporal together is what makes a writer traditional. The past is altered by the present just as the present is formed by the past.'[56] 'The mind of Europe – a mind which he learns in time to be much more important than his own private mind – is a mind which changes, and . . . this change is a development which abandons nothing en route, which does not superannuate either Shakespeare, or Homer, or the rock drawing of the Magdalenian draughtsmen. If it be said that 'the dead writers are remote from us because we know so much more than they did,' the answer is, "Precisely, and they are that which we know".'[57]

When J. A. Smith wrote in 1924 that his dedication to the philosophy of Croce had renewed in him a 'reverential discipleship to the great classics of Modern, Medieval, and Ancient philosophy,' while at the same time it made him ready to sit respectfully at the feet of such recent writers as Bergson, Royce, Bradley, and Bosanquet, he was reflecting an Oxford habit that his Crocean commitment elevated to a principle.[58] The real is History, 'an event which occupies the whole of time, and the same holds every genuine event within it, so that the time of one does not exclude the time of another, but all such times interpenetrate one another,' with the consequence that Mind always attempts more and more adequate expressions of the real 'by an adjustment of the competing claims of successiveness and simultaneity'.[59] The summary function of history became a constant of Eliot's thought. Later he would write that 'no great philosophy ever vanquishes another great philosophy; it annihilates merely its predecessor's degenerate descendents.'[60] This is the habit of mind – Smith would have said the presupposition – that undergirds Eliot's idea of the tradition as a complex whole altered and fulfilled by the new, and of time as summary of the real, or all of tradition. Thus the apodictic 'Time past is time present.'

Eliot would not have discovered the idea of the summary unity of history in either Bradley's early essay *The Presuppositions of Critical History* or in *Appearance and Reality*. Time in the Absolute was unreal, and 'it is a hope doomed only to disappointment, when the present expects in the mind of the past to find the views and beliefs of the present.'[61] History was, as Smith understood, not a category assimilable to the philosophy of the Absolute. In 1914-1915 the organic unity of time as a presupposition for the doing of history was a project of the Smith-Collingwood connection, developed from Crocean themes.

The larger mind of Europe that is more important than individual minds is of course an idea rooted ultimately in Hegel. John Alexander Smith had expressed its Crocean transformation in his inaugural: 'All genuine knowledge is historical – is knowledge of history, and history is as a whole and in every part the achievement of will – not of this or that individual will of this or that individual knower, but in and through their wills of that universal Will which endlessly fulfills its good pleasure, as in their knowing and universal Mind which is allied with its endless review of its achievements, uniting its vision and its volition in the whole and single Life which is Reality.'[62] Bereft of Smith's supererogatory capitalizations, the Crocean idea became in Eliot's hands an explanation of the relation of past to present in a way that transcended the personality of the poet. 'What is to be insisted upon is that the poet must develop or procure the consciousness of the past and that he should continue to develop this consciousness throughout his career. What happens is a continual surrender of himself as he is at the moment to something which is more valuable. The progress of an artist is a continual self-sacrifice, a continual extinction of personality.'[63] Thirty years later Eliot would write of Joseph Pieper: 'His mind is submissive to what he believes to be the great, the main tradition of European thought.'[64]

The idea of the objectivity of tradition would provide a reformed basis for the doing of history by lifting tradition above the subjectivity of the poet while at the same time refuting the idea that we can know the past as past and insisting that we always know it in the context of a complex whole which is the historian's imagination. Eliot would overcome the historicism of nineteenth century criticism by presenting the literary tradition as a complex whole which is contemporary, in which Homer and Dante are our contemporaries. The main idea of 'Tradition and the Individual Talent,' Eliot's thesis that the present incorporates a living past answered the progressivist thesis that because we know so much more the old poets are irrelevant to contemporary experience, and gave the essay its stature as a piece still read by first year students except in those places in which the writ of de-construction runs. Eliot's defense of literary tradition was rooted in his reading of the Greek and Latin texts, accessible to him as it would seldom be to writers of the post-1945 generation.[65] Oxford had impressed upon Eliot, then in Collingwood's *De Anima* seminar, 'the value of careful study of original texts in the original language' in contrast to the synoptic course. Collingwood wrote of the method he had used in 1914-1915: 'I had become something of a specialist in Aristotle, and the first lectures I gave were on the *De Anima*. My plan was to concentrate on the question, 'What is Aristotle saying and what does he mean by it?' and to forgo, however alluring it might be, the further question 'Is it true?' What I wanted to do was to train my audience in the scholarly approach to a philosophical text, leaving on one side, as sufficiently provided for by other teachers, the further business of criticising its doctrine.'[66] The past could form Eliot's imaginal present because he could read its words.

III

In 1917 'Tradition and the Individual Talent' established the historical presupposition of Eliot's criticism, and posited an important theme of his life. Five years later the sudden death of the Professor of Poetry, William Ker, a man Eliot incidentally approved, and the election of Heathcote William Garrod as Ker's successor was to demonstrate the sympathy that linked Eliot's new poetry – the *Waste Land* had been published in 1922 – and the Crocean aesthetic of the New Idealism. Garrod in time-honored style delivered his inaugural in February 1924, taking the occasion to attack the new poetry, which in 1924 meant the *Waste Land*. This poetry, Garrod noted, had one of the requisites for greatness, 'immense faith in itself.' Its roots, he wrote, display 'a freedom believed to be new,' and 'its language affects an extreme plainness, and its content is informed by the dogma that whatever is is good enough for poetry.' 'Its purposes are whatever may be its results; or at any rate its final cause does not stand in ethical theory.' To Garrod the new poets seemed 'almost intolerably trim and brisk.' 'That all this poetry,' he added, 'or most of it, is good I should not like to affirm.'[67] For his part Garrod preferred poetry that scanned, and which displayed 'poetic diction.' He was, Garrod wrote, stuck in two dogmas, that among the purposes of poetry is pleasure, and that 'there is very little in literature or life, that affords permanent pleasure which has not some hold in ethics.'[68] Shakespeare consists of 'words made not for but with music, and the art is dead, and it is a chance if anything like it will again revisit literature. The body of our joy has visibly shrunken.' 'Already we are asking whether it need scan, and yet again whether poetry need be verse at all.' True, at times Garrod came within the orbit of the idea that poetry is self-knowledge. 'The end of poetry is to present life.' 'The poet is, in fact, the prophet of the world's final causes; the interpreter, vexed often and hesitant, but still the only present interpreter, of a creation groaning and travailing after its proper meaning.'[69] But taken together Garrod's inaugural was a depreciation of the new poetry and implicitly of Eliot. For Garrod poetry was didactic and the new professor of poetry was oddly oblivious to the ethical pre-suppositions that lay, unenunciated, within Eliot's image of the small house agent's clerk creeping up the stairs to his neurasthenic assignation.

Smith, who had been his philosophical mentor when Garrod was an undergraduate, did not let the matter alone but, after a long conversation with Garrod during which Smith's worst suspicions were confirmed, published in May, 1924 *The Nature of Art: An Open Letter to the Professor of Poetry in the University of Oxford*, in which, having politely offered the collegial nature of teaching as the warrant for his interference, Smith advanced in rapid sequence against Garrod's rather conventional ideas the dramatic and sometimes paradoxical themes of the Crocean aesthetic. Art is a knowing, not a doing, a knowing of the individual; the universal is precisely what it does not reveal. The arts are one. Art is not an object but a spirit. Art is not a work of will. It sets no end and knows no means to its attainment. Yet it is not a passive knowing, but a knowing that is a seeing. Art does not moralize; the artist does not edify himself or anyone else. Art is not a making, and therefore not an imitation. Art is expression. Art is imagination. Art is and uses language; it is impossible to confine art to what is spoken or written. Art gives thought imaginal body, and in this way unites intellect and imagination.[70]

Professor Garrod responded to Smith's open letter in 'Poets and Philosophers.' Just as Garrod assumed that the absence of ethical assertion deprived the new poetry of morality, he mistakenly saw Smith's Crocean theories as anti-intellectual and his defense of art as a thing individual as a romantic rejection of meaning and intelligibility.[71]

The last point in Smith's refutation of 1924, his Crocean insistence that in poetry imagination and feeling become intelligible and thought becomes feeling, was to be the aesthetic heart of Eliot's Clark Lectures of 1926. The corollary, Eliot's thesis that the spirituality and poetry of early modernity represented a dissociation of sensibilities, became the grounds on which Collingwood would in *Principles of Art* consider the *Waste Land*, sixteen years after its publication, the greatest modern poem. In 1924, the year in which Professor Smith criticized Garrod's inaugural, Collingwood published *Speculum Mentis*, making in it the point that 'a concept can only be conceived, not intuited; to say that a concept exists intuitively, to speak of a meaning fused or identified with its sensuous vehicle, is merely to contradict oneself. And yet this contradiction is the essence of art.'[72] The thesis that in poetry feeling and imagination find an indissoluble unity, the point which Garrod seemingly did not grasp or did not grasp as formulated by Professor Smith, became a matter of controversy just as the Oxford realists in the person of Professor I. A. Richards undertook a defense of the critical theory intrinsic to positivism, a school in which the dissociation of fact and emotion was dogma. In his *Principles of Literary Criticism*, published in 1925, Richards defended the realist aesthetic by arguing (against the Smith-Collingwood thesis that language unites feeling and thought) that language has two uses, one the objective representation of truth, the other emotive.[73] The unity of thought and feeling in language and hence the ability of poetry to give feeling intellectual form, an idea rooted perhaps ultimately in Kant's *Critique of Judgement*, in Coleridge's *Biographia Literaria*, and developed in Croce's *Esthetica* was the fundamental idea of the New Idealism's aesthetic. Richards' counter thesis was rooted in the fact/value disjunction that had made its way from Hume to H. A. Prichard and A. J. Ayer. Poetry might then be emotive but not truth-telling. The emotion of love, Professor Richards had maintained in the *Criterion*, might have no relation at all to its object.[74]

Perhaps the Garrod-Smith controversy was bound to occur at a time when the death of the idea that art is the representation of the beautiful and the emergence of the idea that art is a kind of supra-conceptual truth-telling, an idea with which Ruskin had grappled murkily, had been rendered inevitable by the fact of post-Great War art itself. Gulley Jimson, the hero of Joyce Carey's *Horse's Mouth*, is made to say that his father, like the protagonist a painter, had died of a broken heart when pictures of girls in gardens had suddenly become unpopular as Pre-Raphaelitism swept England. By 1914, under the inspiration of the Impressionists and Post Impressionists, of Whistler and Beardsley, beauty had disappeared as the criterion of art. If truth had been beauty, beauty truth before 1914, the truth about the human condition after 1914 was no longer beautiful, with the consequence that art in its new grotesqueness, significant for the eye of the beholder and expressive of the artist's vision, became, to Garrod's chagrin, the fact with which criticism was required to deal. The function of art as an enterprise capable of giving thought imaginal and emotional form came front and center. Art suddenly increased the range of feelings that could be expressed, enabling the reader to know how it feels to have no coherent philosophy at all.

IV

Chronologically the Clark lectures of 1926 stand between Eliot's unavoidable immersion during his Oxford year in Croce's aesthetic – the *Brevario di estetica* had been published in English in 1912 – and Collingwood's *Principles of Art* (1938). Their theme, whatever its particular aegis, was Crocean: the unity of thought and emotion in poetry and the symptomatic personal and cultural default that must occur when that unity is broken, when thought can no longer be given a poetic body of feeling. The Cambridge lectures have a curious history. They marked Eliot's acceptance as an important critic and the maturing of the mutual approval characteristic of his relations with the Cambridge English School, but a decade later he considered them pretentious, immature and unpublishable, while at the same time he continued to use parts and pieces in other essays, and returned intermittently to tease the idea of publication.[75]

If Eliot's broad thesis was the emotional unity of thought and feeling in some metaphysical poetry, the historical counter-thesis was the progressive dissociation of thought and feeling from the thirteenth century, when Dante, the metaphysical poet supreme, embodied medieval thought, preeminently the philosophy of Aquinas, perfectly in the *Divine Comedy*, through the incipient psychological modernity of the Jesuits and St. Theresa of Avila, to the partially successful experiments of Donne, a modernity in which emotion characteristically fails to engage thought and thought is set adrift from the body of feeling that makes it integral to life. Thought is then disastrously dissociated from feeling, a progress marked by the decline from the ontology of Hugh of St. Victor, for whom the real was God, to the affective piety, the psychology in Eliot's words, of the Jesuits, in whose ascetic life the drama of the self had begun to predominate.[76]

The Clark Lectures display Eliot's extensive reading not only in familiar sources but in a new philosophy, for by 1925 Eliot had read the stalwarts of the Catholic Revival, Jacques Maritain, Etienne Gilson, Maurice De Wulf, Martin D'Arcy, and Cardinal Mercier.[77] Essentially historical in their development, the fruition of that love for the history of thought that Oxford had encouraged in him, Eliot designed the lectures around the historical movement from Dante's poetic engagement with reality to the psychology of Donne and his successors, an historical movement that in Eliot's analysis pointed toward the Cartesian bifurcation of experience into a world of thought and a world of matter, a thesis intrinsic to the intellectual historiography of the French Catholic Revival as Eliot knew it through Maritain and Gilson. Descartes, Eliot believed, who in the sixth *Meditation* had held the existence of the body unproveable, was, if not responsible for the alienation of matter from the intelligible world, at least emblematic of this error, a thesis to which the further conclusion that Descartes's philosophy had underwritten the separation of the world as experienced from the world of thought was a temptingly close analogy.[78]

Eliot's insistence on the unity of thought and feeling in the individual work of art was, like the idea of history that informs 'Tradition and the Individual Talent,' a Crocean theme. Art, Croce had written in the *Brevario*, 'is precisely a yearning kept within the bounds of a representation. In art the yearning [for expression] is there solely for the sake of representation, and representation solely for the sake of the yearning. . . . What we admire is the perfect imaginative form that a state of mind assumes there.'[79] The function of poetry, Eliot wrote, is 'both to fix and make more conscious the precise emotions and feelings in which most people participate in their own experience, and to draw within the orbit of feeling and sense what had existed only in thought. It creates a unity of feeling out of various parts: a unity of action which is epic or dramatic; a union (the simplest form) of sound and sense, the pure lyric; and in various forms the union of things hitherto unconnected in experience.' When Catullus writes his famous lines contrasting the sun, which will rise and set again, with the lot of man, who sleeps one never-ending night, 'he is modifying an emotion by a thought and a thought by an emotion, integrating them into the new emotion, an emotion which with all its variations of subsequent poets, has been experienced, doubtless, by many generations of lovers.'[80]

Not all poetry was in Eliot's sense metaphysical, yet 'in certain periods the revolution of the sphere of thought will so to speak throw off ideas which will fall within the attraction of poetry. It is these moments of history when human sensibility is momentarily enlarged in certain directions, that I propose to call the metaphysical periods.'[81] In these moments poetry 'elevates sense for a moment to regions ordinarily attainable only by abstract thought, or, on the other hand, clothes the abstract , for the moment, with all the painful delight of flesh. I wish to emphasize the intellectual quality of this operation of poetry.'[82]

Thus poetry was not only useful but indispensable, adding to human expreience in two ways: 'One is by perceiving and recording accurately the world – of both sense and feeling – as given at any moment. The other is by extending the frontier of this world.'[83] The Clark lectures are the poet's rendering of the thesis that poetry tells the truth, not propositionally, but the truths of our feelings or as Collingwood would later say, the secrets of our hearts.[84] Hence art becomes a means not to pleasure or beauty, although these may befall us, but a way of telling and knowing the truth, and the inability of thought to discover a poetic body of feeling is a cultural storm warning.

V

The Croce-Smith tradition at Oxford, effectively the New Idealism, attained its ultimate expression in Collingwood's *Principles of Art* in 1938, and in that work the practice of poetry by Eliot and the idealist aesthetic found their consonance, the poet and the philosopher returning as it were to important if unacknowledged themes of Smith's informals and common room conversations of 1914-1915.

The concluding paragraphs of *Principles of Art* are important and remarkable because in them Collingwood enunciates his mature theory of the use of poetry, a development of ideas Eliot had proposed in 1926, illustrating this use through an emotionally charged appeal to 'one great poet' who had abandoned the attempt to write 'pure literature,' setting the example of what poetry should be by writing about 'a subject that interests everyone,' the decay of our civilization.[85] Implicit in Collingwood's praise is the assumption that poetry has a use. In those paragraphs Collingwood acknowledges what he knew were Eliot's critical principles by noting that in the *Waste Land* there is 'no question of expressing private emotions,' agreeing with Eliot's critical view that poetry is about neither the poet's own emotions or the poet's biography. Nor is the poem a moral tale containing indictments and edifying proposals. It is not amusing; not, as neo-Kiplings would claim, political. The *Waste Land*, Collingwood wrote, is indeed not representative of any romantic or personal theory of the use of poetry, and was of course not made with any purpose other than itself. And yet poetry has a use, of which the *Waste Land* is the great example, a use important to the intellectual armory of Collingwood at the zenith of his fighting philosopher stage. Art, specifically poetry, specifically this poem, is 'the community's medicine for the worst disease of mind, the corruption of consciousness.'[86]

So having written two hundred pages about what art is and is not, much of which is calculated to deny that it does anything, that in the common language of the school art has anything at all to do with the practical will, Collingwood asserts that poetry does have one use: it is a consummate act of self knowledge, telling the audience the secrets of their own hearts, providing the cure for that inability to render feelings into images thereby knowing them and knowing oneself. This theory of the use of poetry is as new as poetic modernism; it is not to be found in Coleridge, or Hackett, or Dryden or Arnold.

Eliot is, not once but twice, the 'one great poet' who in his *Waste Land* has pursued this purpose, illustrating thereby the aesthetic of *Principles of Art*. Collingwood's defense of the use of poetry as a truth-telling image and of Eliot's poetry as exemplary, like their common defense of the unity of thought and feeling in poetry, are characteristic inventions of the New Idealism of the twenties, a movement which Collingwood and Eliot shared, a movement rooted immediately in Croce, remotely in Bradley or even Coleridge, but more particularly in the Oxford of the decade after 1909, in the thought of John Alexander Smith, who combined Crocean themes with English Idealism and propagandized this heady brew in lectures, essays, letters, at philosophers' teas, and in countless conversations.

The movement of both Eliot and Collingwood from the theoretical defense of the unity of thought and feeling in poetry to the note of alarm at the consequences of poetic failure to achieve this unity presupposes the Croce-Smith idea of the use of history in its close relation to their systematic aesthetic. Croce had since 1893 linked art and history because these are the characteristically imaginative, aesthetic activities. The nature of art, any kind of art, as a means to self-knowledge is rooted in the doing of history and depends upon the philosophy of self-knowledge or self-making characteristic of the idea of history intrinsic to the New Idealism. When Collingwood twice in *Principles of Art* praises Eliot because he never wrote a line of pure poetry, that is, never a line of poetry which was merely formal, purely self-referential, structuralist, he is reminding the reader that after two hundred printed pages in which he has told us much that art is not, and some things that it is, there remains a use of poetry which presupposes history, the super-personal history of Eliot's 'Tradition and the Individual Talent' that affords more than personal insight. The Smith-Croce theory of history underlies not only Eliot's understanding of tradition, but a certain understanding of the doing of history as the making of that self who feels and thinks, the historian of Collingwood's 'Human Nature and Human History'. Collingwood is also reminding us that Collingwood himself never wrote a line of pure history in which the historian began his task with a self-consciousness contentless and absolutely free. The making and knowing of art, which is analogous to the making of the self and to self knowledge, is rooted in the doing of history. Schuchard cites Christopher Ricks as one familiar with Eliot's 'profoundest sense of what creation is: the creation of one's self, and the creation of others' selves, in society and in procreation and through and within art's imaginings.'[87] Since philosophy is fundamentally the doing of history, which is the development of the self or of self-consciousness, and since art is, in another way, the artist's coming to self-knowledge and the expression of that self-knowledge in a way that shows the audience its own heart, the content of the history and art thus made will be the philosophical content of consciousness and will show us the truth, the disease and its cure. Post-impressionist art is the image, and history the story, of the modern failure of self-knowledge, a failure predicated upon or occasioned by the dissociation of sensibility, the failure of sense and thought to discover their proper unity in feeling. What in fact the development of the idea of poetry as knowledge and more specifically as self-knowledge, an idea posited philo-sophically in Croce's *Aesthetic*, John Alexander Smith's *The Nature of Art*, and Collingwood's *Principles of Art*, which is exemplified in Eliot's critical theory, has proposed to modern literary criticism is a significant non-pragmatic, non-analytic principle. In the Collingwood-Eliot theory of the uses of art two theses of the New Idealism were joined: the theme of history as the making of the self and the idea that the failure of that making involved the failure of persons and civilizations to unite thought and feeling, a failure, or success, with respect to which art is emblematic, diagnostic, and therapeutic.

One might note finally that the Smith-Collingwood-Eliot aesthetic represented the inferential reassertion of assumptions rooted in the pre-history of modern European philosophy. For fifteen centuries European art had been iconic, images in which truth was rendered positively, often beautifully, but as art became secular, artists inevitably played with the separation of the implied, ideal ground of significance from the aesthetic surface of art and poetry, a surface necessarily derived from and located in the world of experience, creating a tension between the image conceived formally and its implied ground, between feeling and thought. Then suddenly, like a boat heeled by the wind one degree too much, the formality that truth must be imaginally significant, which had been the matrix of meaning, became an invariable, aesthetically suppressed implicate located in the intellectual background, while the aesthetic surface took up the ugly, the chaotic, the terrifying. Picasso's women would not work unless beauty were the background, and Munch's frightening figure emerging from the subway would not terrify unless we had some better ordered vision. This ugliness is good art because it tells us the secrets of our hearts, how our thoughts in fact feel and what meanings our feelings encapsulate. The cost of bad art, art that in practice denies that these images make emotionally intelligible our feelings about the world, is that failure of art Collingwood called corruption of consciousness and Eliot the dissociation of sensibility.

NOTES

1 Benedetto Croce, *Guide to Aesthetics*, trans. Patrick Romanell (South Bend, Indiana: Regnery/Gateway, 1979), 25.
2 *Lectures on the Metaphysical Poetry of the Seventeenth Century with special reference to Donne, Crashaw, and Cowley, delivered at Trinity College Cambridge 1926*, in Ronald Schuchard, ed. *The Varieties of Metaphysical Poetry* (New York: Harcourt Brace & Company, 1993), 103.
3 R. G. Collingwood, *Principles of Art* (Oxford: Clarendon Press, 1938), 295.
4 On Bradley's influence, or lack of influence, see Thompson, 27-30; Richard Schusterman, *T. S. Eliot and the Philosophy of Criticism* (New York: Columbia University Press, 1988), 14-15, 195; Richard Wollheim, *F. H. Bradley* (Harmondsworth, U.K.: Penguin, 1969); and especially Jeffrey M. Perl, *Skepticism and Modern Enmity: Before and After Eliot* (Baltimore: Johns Hopkins University Press, 1989). References to Croce occur in the somewhat unlikely

context of Collingwood's *De Anima* lectures [Aristotelis *De Anima, libri tres,* Translation and Commentary, Collingwood Papers. Bodlean]. Collingwood noted that 'the ms. is intended to cover 2 hours a week for 8 weeks given in 1913 and enlarged in 1914.'

5 Alan Donagan, *The Later Philosophy of R. G. Collingwood: A Critical Study* (Oxford: University Press, 1962); Eric Thompson, *T. S. Eliot: The Metaphysical Perspective* (Carbondale: Southern Illinois University Press, 1963); Guido Vanheeswijck, 'R. G. Collingwood, T. S. Eliot, and the Romantic Tradition,' *Collingwood Studies* III (1996), 76-96.

6 G. Dawes Hicks considered J. A. Smith the founder of the New Idealism [*Hibbert Journal* 38 (1939-40), 401-402]. See James Patrick, *The Magdalen Metaphysicals* (Macon, Georgia: Mercer University Press, 1984), xxiv, note 27.

7 Louis Freed, *T. S. Eliot: The Critic as Philosopher* (West Lafayette, Indiana: Purdue University Press, 1979), xviii.

8 John Alexander Smith, 'Philosophy as the Development of the Notion and Reality of Self-Consciousness,' in J. H. Muirhead, ed. *Contemporary British Philosophy.* Ser. 2 (London: Allen and Unwin, 1924), 231. On Joachim's election see J. A. Smith to F. S. Marvin, 3 July 1919 [Bodleian MSS, MS. Eng, lett.c.482]; Eliot to Woods. 20 February 1916, *The Letters of T. S. Eliot.* Volume I: 1898-1922. Valerie Eliot, ed. (San Diego: Harcourt Brace Jovanovich, 1988), 132 [Hereinafter *Letters.*]

9 Collingwood Diary, June 9, October 30, and November 3, Collection of Teresa Collingwood Smith [Hereinafter TCS]. Smith praised Collingwood's translation of Croce's *Vico* in his review of H. Wilson Carr, *The Philosophy of Benedetto Croce: The Philosophy of Art and History [Hibbert Journal* 16 (1916), 505]; and provided the preface to Collingwood's translation of Croce's *An Autobiography* (Oxford: Clarendon Press, 1927). Smith thanked Collingwood for doing much of his work for him in a letter of 30 January 1938, John Alexander Smith Papers, Magdalen College Archives [Hereinafter SPM]. E. W. F. Tomlin [*R. G. Collingwood* (London: Longmans, Green, 1957), 18] cites Smith's influence in securing the Waynflete chair for Collingwood.

10 Collingwood, Diary, July 12, 1917 [TCS].

11 Nicholas Griffin, ed., *The Selected Letters of Bertrand Russell: Volume I: The Private Years, 1884-1914* (Boston: Houghton Mifflin, 1992), 230, 3n; R. F. Harrod, *The Prof: A Personal Memoir of Lord Cherwell* (London: Macmillan, 1959), 21; Paul Elmer More to Alice More, 4 November, 1924, quoted in Arthur Hazard Dakin, *Paul Elmer More* (Princeton, New Jersey: Princeton University Press, 1960), 225; R. G. Collingwood, *Autobiography* (Oxford: University Press, 1939), 18. 14. C. S. Lewis, *An Allegory of Love* (Oxford: University Press, 1936), vii; Josiah Royce to Ralph Barton Perry, John Clendenning, ed., *The Letters of Josiah Royce* (Chicago: University of Chicago Press, 1970), 591.

12 Typical are Schusterman, who mentions only Eliot's study of Aristotle with Joachim., and William Skaff, *The Philosophy of T. S. Eliot: From Skepticism to a Surrealistic Poetic, 1909-1922* (Philadelphia: University of Pennsylvania Press, 1986), who ignores the Oxford year. In *The Magdalen Metaphysicals,* written before publication of the Clark Lectures or the *Letters,* I failed to develop the influence of Croce on Eliot (148-150). Freed's treatment of the resonances between Joachim's philosophy and Eliot's is a noteworthy exception (xviii, 14, 29, 78, 104, 159-62)

13 John Brett Langstaff, *Oxford 1914* (New York: Vantage, 1965), 256.

14 'Hegel I rather dipped into and occasionally consulted than read,' 'Philosophy,' 229.

15 28 December 1915 [*Letters,* 124]. Collingwood, remembering his own undergradute years, wrote in 1938 of the school of T. H. Green, 'the best of them were J. A. Smith, who

had been a pupil of Nettleship, and H. H. Joachim, a close personal friend of Bradley' [*Autobiography*, 18].

16 Eliot, *Lectures*, 82; Schuchard, 'Eliot and Hulme in 1916: Toward a Revaluation of Eliot's Critical and Spiritual Development,' *P.M.L.A.*, LXXXVIII (1973), 1083-94. In 1909-1910 Eliot had taken Babbit's 'Literary Criticism in France with Special Reference to the Nineteenth Century.'

17 John D. Margolis [*T. S. Eliot's Intellectual Development 1922-1939* (Chicago: University of Chicago Press, 1972)] notes the early influence of Charles Maurras. Before October 1916, when Maurras was recommended in Eliot's extension lectures syllabus, and probably during the academic year 1913-14, when he had taken Babbit's Harvard seminar, Eliot had read Maurras' *L'Avenir de l'intelligence* and *La Politique Religieus*, as well as Charles Sorel's *Reflections on Violence*. See 'Syllabus of a Course of Six Lectures on Modern French Literature' in Schuchard, 'Eliot as an Extension Lecturer, 1916-1919,' Part I, *Review of English Studies* n.s. 25 (May 1974), 167. On the influence of the Harvard faculty on Eliot see Manju Jain, *T. S. Eliot and American Philosophy* (Cambridge: University press, 1992), which includes a schedule of Eliot's undergraduate and graduate courses.

18 T. S. Eliot, Preface to Josef Pieper, *Leisure the Basis of Culture* (New York: Pantheon, 1952) Eliot wrote Eleanor Hinkley [21 March 1915] that although he enjoyed talking with Russell, 'he has a sensitive but not really a cultivated mind, and I begin to realize how unbalanced he is.' T. S. Eliot, *Knowledge and Experience in the Philosophy of F. H. Bradley* (New York: Farrar , Strauss, 1964), 84-140; Brand Blanshard, 'Eliot in Memory,' *Yale Review* 54 (1964-65), 637.

19 Josiah Royce and F. H. Bradley 'presented arguments which , I suggest, altered Eliot's intellect, drawing it into the idealist tradition' [Piers Gray, *T. S. Eliot's Intellectual and Poetic Development, 1909-1922* (Sussex: Harvester, 1982), 90-174]. Eliot would have known something of Oxford philosophy and philosophers from R. F. Alfred Hoernle, whose Seminary in Metaphysics Eliot attended in Fall 1913. Eliot's unpublished 'Comments on T. H. Green's Metaphysics and Ethics' [Hayward Bequest, Kings College Library, Cambridge] argues his familiarity with the Idealist tradition at its source.

20 Eliot to Norbert Wiener, 6 January 1915 [*Letters*, 79].

21 Eliot, *Knowledge and Experience*, 153.

22 Eliot to William C. Greene, 14 October 1914 [*Letters*, 66].

23 9 November 1914 [*Letters*, 67].

24 9 November 1914 [*Letters*, 68].

25 28 January 1915. Eliot still had not sent his *De Anima* notes in March 1917, when he explained to Woods that they were on interleaves 'and in such small writing that I fear no one could possibly decipher them but myself. I do not quite like to trust the fruit of so much labour to the submarines in the Channel' (23 March, 1917).

26 6 May 1915, Stewart was of course the great classicist; William McDougall was the Wilde Lecturer in mental philosophy, representative of the attempt of Oxford Idealism to find an effective alternative to John Watson's behaviorism.

27 John Burnet, 27 February 1910, in the *Letter of Application to the Electors to the Waynflete Chair of Moral and Metaphysical Philosophy*, printed privately at Oxford, March 1910.

28 A. J. Ayer, *Part of My Life* (London: Collins, 1977), 77.

29 R. G. Collingwood, *The Idea of History* (Oxford: University Press, 1946), 190-204.

30 Croce's contention that in order to write history one must experience the inside of history, knowing it subjectively as did the historical subjects who made it, is the genesis of Collingwood's doctrine of reenactment. The notion that ideas must be experienced or

felt, is closely analogous to Eliot's thesis that in proper self-consciousness ideas and feelings are coordinate.

31 *Letters*, xxi.

32 Minutes of the Pembroke philosophy club, 1923; R.G. Collingwood, *Autobiography*, 44-51.

33 Eliot to Mrs. Jack Gardner, 10? July? 1915 [*Letters*, 107]; Charlotte C. Eliot to Bertrand Russell, 18 January 1916 [*Letters*, 130-131].

34 T. S. Eliot, *The Sacred Wood* (London: Methuen, 1920), 12.

35 Eliot, *Sacred Wood*, 9.

36 Eliot to Norbert Wiener, 6 January 1915 [*Letters*, 79]. In 1913 Eliot, wrestling with the problem of the truth of interpretations, concluded an argument with the assertion, 'You can't understand me. To understand my point of view, you have to believe it first.' H. T. Costello, 'Recollections of Royce's Seminar on Comparative Methodology,' *Journal of Philosophy*, LIII (February 2, 1956), 76.

37 Eliot to Norbert Wiener, 6 January 1915 [*Letters*, 80].

38 Eliot, Preface to Pieper, *Leisure the Basis of Culture*, 13.

39 Eliot's mature philosophic position was significantly influenced by the continental and English Catholic Revival philosophers who, following Leo XIII's recommendation that the study of the patristic and scholastic sources, and especially of St. Thomas, be pursued, recovered the ideal of an organic relation between philosophy and theology, grace and nature, reason and revelation; and created a distinctive historiography in which the unity of the tradition was emphasized and the origins of modernity traced to Ockham and Descartes. See Schuchard, ed., Clark Lectures, 77; T. S. Eliot, Review of Jacques Maritain, *Three Reformers*. TLS 1397 (8 November 1928) 818; Review of Maurice de Wulf, *History of Medieval Philosophy*, TLS (16 December 1926), 929. J. Hillis Miller [*Poets of Reality* (Cambridge; Harvard University Press, 1965), 129-30] discusses Eliot's passage from the Bradlean 'wilderness of mirrors' into a philosophy that assumed the objective existence of a world.

40 Eliot, Preface to Pieper, *Leisure the Basis of Culture*, 14.

41 T. S. Eliot, Review of William Temple, *Mens Creatrix*, *International Journal of Ethics* XXVII, no. 4 (July 1917), 542-43; Review of R. G. Collingwood, *Speculum Mentis*, *International Journal of Ethics*, XXVII. no. 4 (July 1917), 543. Eliot's view of Christianity as based upon a set of discrete facts, an idea that flew in the face of the characteristic English theology of the Edwardian and immediate post-war period, was an idea that, as Eliot noted, always separated his own thought from that of the idealists. While Eliot was increasingly insistent on the historicity of the Christian account, Collingwood was part of the B. H. Streeter group, Oxford dons and fellow travelers dedicated to rendering Christianity acceptable because philosophic. Collingwood's treatment of the Christian religion rescues it from psychology but never elevates it beyond philosophy.

42 Eliot to Mary Hutchinson, 22 September, 1920 [*Letters*, 409]

43 Review of M. C. D'Arcy, *The Nature of Belief*, in *Criterion* 11(1931-32), 334-336; Review of Charles Gore, *The Philosophy of the Good Life* in *Criterion* 10(1930-31), 560-562.

44 T. S. Eliot, 'Rudyard Kipling,' *On Poetry and Poets* 279n; Collingwood, *Principles of Art*, 333.

45 A. E. Dodds, Review of *The Use of Poetry and the Use of Criticism: Studies in the Relation of Criticism to Poetry in England*. The Charles Eliot Norton Lectures for 1932-1933, by T. S. Eliot (Cambridge: University Press, 1933), in *Modern Language Notes* LI (January-December 1936), 51.

46 Eliot to Woods. 2 March 1915 [*Letters*, 89]. Eliot's assessment of Oxford was various.

He did not relish university life, preferring London, but Eliot did quite consciously admire and appropriate the then common method of reading texts closely and in the original language and the characteristically Oxfordian interest in the history of philosophy.

47 C. S. Lewis, *Pilgrim's Regress* (Grand Rapids, Michigan: Wm. B. Eerdmans, 1958), 5; Leonard Woolf, *Downhill All the Way: An Autobiography of the Years 1919-1939* (London: Hogarth press, 1967), 28.

48 Smith, 'Philosophy', 236.

49 'The Theory of History,' SPM, II,4. The author was quoting Smith, 'The Contribution of Greece and Rome,' in F. S. Marvin, *The Unity of Western Civilization* (London: Humphrey Milford, 1915), 69, and Smith was reciting a Crocean commonplace (90).

50 Smith, 'The Contribution of Greece and Rome,' 69.

51 Smith, 'Ancient Philosophy,' SPM, IV,8.

52 Smith, 'The Contribution of Greece and Rome,' 72

53 Smith, Preface to Benedetto Croce, *An Autobiography*, tr. R. G. Collingwood (Oxford: Clarendon Press, 1927), 17-18.

54 Smith, 'Philosophy', 236, cf. 232.

55 Collingwood, *Idea of History*, 226.

56 'Tradition and the Individual Talent,' in *Selected Essays* (New York: Harcourt Brace, 1932), 4.

57 Eliot, 'Tradition and the Individual Talent,' 6.

58 Smith, 'Philosophy,' 233.

59 Smith, 'Philosophy,' 236.

60 Eliot, 'Tradition and the Individual Talent,' 6-7. Cf. John Alexander Smith, 'Knowing and Acting', An Inaugural Lecture delivered before the University of Oxford, 26 November 1910', rpt. *Oxford Lectures on Philosophy, 1910-23* (Freeport, New York: Books for Library Press, 1969), 10.

61 F. H. Bradley, *Presuppositions of Critical History* (Oxford: J. Parker, 1874); rpt. ed. Lionell Rubinoff (Toronto: J. M. Dent, 1968), 117.

62 Smith, 'Knowing and Acting,' 29.

63 Eliot, 'Tradition and the Individual Talent,' 7.

64 Eliot, Preface to Pieper, 15.

65 Blanshard, ['Eliot in Memory,' 634-35] cites testimonies to Eliot's mastery of the classical languages.

66 Collingwood, *Autobiography.* 27

67 Heathcote William Garrod, 'The Profession of Poetry,' delivered February 13, 1924, rpt. *The Profession of Poetry and Other Lectures*, (Oxford: Clarendon Press, 1929), 3.

68 Garrod, 'The Profession of Poetry,' 4.

69 Garrod, 'The Profession of Poetry,' 6.

70 (Oxford, Clarendon Press, 1924). The Smith-Garrod debate was reported in the *Times* by A. W. Walkley, and published in his *Still More Prejudice* (London: William Heinemann, 1925), 49-53.

71 Garrod, 'Poets and Philosophers,' *The Profession of Poetry and Other Essays,* 25-27.

72 R. G. Collingwood, *Speculum Mentis* (Oxford: Clarendon Press, 1924), 89.

73 I. A. Richards, *Principles of Literary Criticism* (1925; rpt. San Diego: Haarcourt Brace Jovanovich, 1985), 267.

74 I. A. Richards, 'A Background for Contemporary Poetry,' *Criterion* (July 1925) 521. Eliot cites this point in the Clark Lectures [Schuchard, ed., 81].

75 Schuchard, ed., 21-26.

76 See note 36 supra. In the Clark Lectures [77 and 77, n33] Eliot cited with approval Gilson's *La Philosophie au moyen age* as a little book that made possible our understanding of the Middle Ages, and of a philosophy which had the advantages of a common belief and of the liberty which the Church afforded. See also Eliot's use of Gilson's *Saint Thomas D'Aquin* (104, and 23n). Eliot commended both these works in 'Medieval Philosophy,' [*TLS* 1298 (10 December 1926), 929], which was contemporary with the Clark Lectures, a review of Maurice De Wulf's *History of Medieval Philosophy*, noting that De Wulf's work was 'a link between the work of Gilson, which consists in detailed exposition of the ideas of the principal philosophers of the thirteenth century in his books on St. Thomas and St. Bonaventure and the massive *Modern Scholastic Philosophy* of Cardinal Mercier.'

77 The Descartes thesis was reiterated in Maritain's *Three Reformers*, which Eliot had read before his *Criterion* review of 1928, and earlier in Gilson's *La philosophie au moyen age*, which Eliot cites in the Clark Lectures of 1926 (Schuchard, ed., 77).

78 Schuchard, ed, 80-81.

79 Croce, *Guide to Aesthetics*, 25. Eliot published an English translation of Croce's *On the Nature of Allegory* (1922) in the April 1925 *Criterion* and Schuchard (*Metaphysical Poetry*, 277) believed he had 'had probably read Croce's *The Poetry of Dante*, 1922).

80 Schuchard, ed., 51.

81 Schuchard, ed., 52-53.

82 Schuchard, ed., 55.

83 Schuchard. ed., 95.

84 Collingwood, *Principles of Art, 333*.

85 Collingwood, *Principles of Art*, 334-335.

86 Collingwood, *Principles of Art*, 336

87 Schuchard, citing Christopher Rick [*The Force of Poetry* (Oxford: Clarendon Press, 1984), 414], 35.

Collingwood's Developing Aesthetic: Artists and Audiences

Donald S. Taylor
University of Oregon

Between 1923 and 1937 R. G. Collingwood's conception of the role of the audience in art, music, and literature underwent radical changes. In *Speculum Mentis,* his earliest extended consideration of the subject, art is an imaginative activity, shared unequally by artists and their audiences. The perceptible work of art – the written or printed poem, painting, score, performance – is, for the artist, instrumental only, entirely secondary, but it is essential for the audience: '. . . the work of art in this false sense, the perceptible painting or writing, is valued not at all by its author, but highly by the aesthetic weakling, because it helps him to aesthetic activities which he could not have achieved alone.'[1]

A year later, in *Outlines of a Philosophy of Art,* the aesthetic weakling has gained a little dignity:

> . . . the life of the imagination is a life in which all human beings participate. . . . The artist does not paint for an audience, but for himself. . . . But what he is trying to satisfy in himself is . . . that imaginative activity which is the same in himself as in others. . . . It is the implicit conviction of this truth that impels the artist to publish or exhibit his works, and to attach some importance to their reception.[2]

The reader or viewer who has understood the work has made an aesthetic advance with the artist's help. 'Genius is the active or creative faculty, taste the passive or receptive; but they are . . . two correlative phases of the same aesthetic activity. . . . Yet there is a real gulf between them, the eternal gulf between master and pupil. . . .' (82) Out of the gymnasium and into the classroom.

The pupil will not come fully into his own until *Principles of Art,* written in 1937. And before this can happen, Collingwood's conception of history as the imaginative reenactment of past thought must make its appearance. In *Outlines* the possibility of such reenactment in literature is explicitly denied.

> . . . this resurrection of ancient art . . . is not a renewal of the past. That is impossible. We may read Chaucer with enjoyment, but we cannot be Chaucer. . . . A work whose greatness in its own day consisted in its paradoxical audacity is enjoyed today for its innocent conventionality by people who detest audacity and paradox. . . . (99)[3]

In 1926, in his essay 'The Place of Art in Education,' reenactment of artistic thought is seen as possible but not desirable: '. . . the words which we read are only the historical record of Shakespeare's literary activity and our reading of them . . . is a literary activity of our own in which Shakespeare's activity lives again, however distorted or diminished by the difference or inferiority of our own mind relatively to Shakespeare's.' Collingwood sees such reenactment as 'restraining, not stimulating, our own imaginative activity.'[4]

By 1928 Collingwood has embraced the idea of reenactment, at least for the historian. In *Outlines of a Philosophy of History*[5] he approaches the concept as he discusses the problems of the historian of 'old music.'

> He must have listened to Bach and Mozart, Palestrina and Lasso. . . . This means that he must have been present at actual performances of these works, either physically or in imagination. . . . . . . the *sine qua non* of writing the history of past music is to have this past music re-enacted in the present. Just the same thing is true of the other arts. . . . (441)

In this statement the difference between historically accurate performances in the present and performances 'in imagination' is not explained, but Collingwood goes on to say that 'in all cases where the history in question is the history of thought, a literal reenactment of the past is possible and is an essential element in all history.' If art is thought, it can be reenacted in the minds of the audience. (444)[6]

In the same lecture the differences in the necessary immediacies of reenactment appear in an artistic context. '. . . the historian of poetry, reading Dante, re-enacts the medieval experience which the poem expresses: but . . . he remains a modern man, not a medieval: . . . the medievalism of Dante, while genuinely revived and re-experienced within his mind, is accompanied by a whole world of fundamentally non-medieval habits and ideas.' The modern context is essential. (447) The Chaucer problem has disappeared.

The reenactment concept is most fully developed eight years later in Collingwood's 1936 lecture 'History as Re-enactment of Past Experience.'[7] Reenactment is here primarily discussed as the necessary mode of the historian's investigations.

> . . . suppose he is reading an . . . ancient philosopher. . . . he must know the language in a philological sense and be able to construe; but . . . he has not yet understood . . . . he must see what the philosophical problem was, of which his author is here stating the solution. . . . This means rethinking for him-self the thought of the author. (283)

Here Collingwood has added the problem-solution, question-answer aspect of thought to his concept of reenactment. Both Hans Robert Jauss and Wolfgang Iser acknowledge the influence of this idea on their own think-ing about aesthetic reception.[8]

A year after this 1936 lecture about reenactment Collingwood wrote *Principles of Art,*[9] which gives us his final position on the idea of audience reenactment. In *Principles* the audience is initially seen, again, as overhearing artists whose expressive acts are their way of understanding their own emotions. But a footnote promises that a more intimate collaboration will be argued in the last two chapters. Long before these chapters, how-ever, the overhearing audience reaches an almost intimate partnership with artists.

. . . when someone reads and understands a poem . . . he is
expressing emotions of his own in the poet's words. As Coleridge
put it, we know a man for a poet by the fact that he makes us
poets . . . . . . the reader is an artist as well as the writer. . . . The
poet is . . . singular in his ability to take the initiative in expressing
what all feel, and all can express. (118-19)

Here the imaginative reenactor, though a follower, has become an artist,
following Collingwood's unchanging conviction that all of us must be
artists.

The audience's response becomes more explicitly reconstructive when
Collingwood turns to musical scores and performances. '. . . what is written
or printed on music pages is not the tune. It is only something which
when studied intelligently will enable others . . . to construct the tune for
themselves in their own heads.' (135) Likewise performances: 'The noises
made by the performers . . . are not the music at all; they are only means
by which the audience, if they listen intelligently (not otherwise) can
reconstruct for themselves the imaginary tune. . . .' (139) Not only must
we imagine the imagined work by means of the heard performance; we
must 'disimagine' extraneous distractions – audience and street noises,
reflective glare on paintings, for example '. . . the conclusion has already
been stated by Shakespeare's Theseus: "the best in this kind . . . are but
shadows, and the worst are no worse if imagination amend them." The
music to which we listen is not the heard sound, but the sound as amended
by the listener's imagination, and so with the other arts.' (162-63)

The whole train of thought in the first book of *Principles* follows from
the foundational premises of Collingwood's philosophy of art: the
universality of artistic activity, the priority of expressive imaginative activity
over the physical 'work of art,' and the necessity, for audiences as well as
historians, of imaginative reenactment.

The second book of *Principles* presents Collingwood's theory of
imagination and concludes with a chapter on language, which 'comes into
existence with imagination.' (225) In this chapter there is an anticipation
of Wolfgang Iser's explanation of gaps and blanks in literary texts, gaps
which the intelligently imagining reader fills.[10] Collingwood writes, 'The
written or printed book is only a series of hints, as elliptical as the neumes

of Byzantine music, from which the reader thus works out for himself the speech gestures which alone have the gift of expression.' (243) Iser sees the gaps as leaving space to be filled by the reader's imagining of incident, thought, expressive elements, and so on, whereas Collingwood is here speaking about print as demanding that the audience imagine tone, emphasis, and gesture, the expressiveness of audible speech. In the unpublished essay 'Words and Tune' (1918)[11] he discusses more fully the 'musical' gaps left to the reader in a written or printed poem. Both Collingwood and Iser are arguing, however, that important elements are left to the reader, and that without the reader's imagining the work is not fully realized. And could not Collingwood's brilliant Byzantine simile be justly extended to cover such techniques as irony, for example, where it is of the essence that the author omit what the reader's imagination must supply. For another example, note what Collingwood's two lectures on Jane Austen[12] praise in Shakespeare and Austen – the loving presentation of glorious fools without authorial denunciation or adjudication; these are left to the reader.

Principles of Art next approaches the artist-audience relationship in an account of the phenomenology of speaking and listening. '. . . the expression of speech contains in itself in principle the experience of speaking to others and of hearing others speak to me.' (248-49) 'The hearer . . . conscious that he is being addressed by another person like himself . . . takes what he hears exactly as if it were speech of his own: he speaks to himself with the words that he hears addressed to him, and thus constructs in himself the idea which these words express.' (250)

This raises a problem. Collingwood notes that there can 'never be any absolute assurance, either for the speaker or the hearer, that the one has understood the other.' However, 'If they understand each other well enough to go on talking, they understand each other as well as they need; and there is no better kind of understanding which they can regret not having attained.' (250-51) This idea, since a commonplace of critical theory, implies a like relative assurance in the conversation between reader and text: the reader imagines and the text then further invites such a reader to go on imagining. In Collingwood's view there are always partial understandings and, as we shall see, multiple legitimate understandings.

At this point reenactment appears explicitly. 'The possibility of such understanding depends on the hearer's ability to reconstruct in his own

consciousness the idea expressed by the words he hears. This reconstruction is an act of imagination; and it cannot be performed unless
the hearer's experience has equipped him for it.' (251) This experience
is the context, the immediacy which reenactment requires.

In the penultimate chapter of *Principles*, 'The Artist and the Community,' Collingwood faces a question which everything he has argued
thus far inevitably raises. 'If the bodily and perceptible 'work of art' is
unnecessary to aesthetic experience in the case of the artist, why should it
be necessary in the case of the audience?' (302) This would imply, first,
a technical theory of art for the audience (the sort of theory denounced at
the outset of *Principles*), but, second, for the artist only, the expressive
theory the book advances throughout.

The answer involves Collingwood in a reconsideration of the function
of the physical, perceptible 'work of art' for the artist. The painter paints
in order to see: the physical painting is vital to the development of the
painter's imaginative experience.

> Every imaginative experience is a sensuous experience raised to the
> imaginative level by an act of consciousness; or, every imaginative
> experience is a sensuous experience together with consciousness
> of the same. . . . Nevertheless, there is always a distinction between
> what transmutes (consciousness), what is transmuted (sensation),
> and what it is transmuted into (imagination). (306-7)

In the case of a painter, the transmuted element is the act of painting,
'the total sensuous (or rather, sensuous-emotional) experience of a man
at work before his easel.' (307) The physical painting 'records' this act. We
can assume that, for Collingwood, the sensuous-emotional work of painting
is analogous to the author's working with words, the composer's working
with sounds, and so on.

These records are as essential to the imagining audience as is the act
of painting to the painter's seeing. '. . . the picture . . . produces in [the
viewer] . . . experiences which, when raised from impressions to ideas by
the activity of the spectator's consciousness, are transmuted into a total
imaginative experience identical with that of the painter.' (308) Here the
audience is active indeed: we have been brought to a point previously

reached by another route. 'Identical' here is then qualified. 'We can never absolutely know that the imaginative experience . . . is identical with that of the artist. In proportion as the artist is a great one, we can be pretty certain that we have only caught his meaning partially and imperfectly.' (309)

The audience's work is not simple. Understanding a work of art 'is always a complex business. A determined and intelligent audience will penetrate into this complex far enough . . . to get something of value; but it need not on that account think it has extracted "the" meaning of the work, for there is no such thing.' Aquinas's doctrine of a plurality of scriptural meanings 'is true of all language' (311) and for Collingwood all art is language.

We have arrived at the position that artists and audiences collaborate in the sense that each work of art is realized anew in each imaginative re-enactment, and that without such reenactment the continued life of the work is only a possibility. At this point in Collingwood's analysis of audience collaboration, something rather puzzling occurs. Chapter fourteen, section five, 'The Audience as Collaborator,' urges that artists – no longer dupes of the romantic notion of the unique genius – take their audiences into account in what they write, paint, compose. Undoubtedly many artists do this, but it does shift the ground from intelligent and expressive conversation with audiences to a matter of the artist's perceptions of an audience's wishes and concerns, to, that is, a more one-sided situation in which the artists shape their works by what they feel their audiences want. They become spokesmen for the audiences they perceive. It is no longer a speaker-listener conversation governed by any sort of conversational reciprocity. It is moving closer to the Aristotelian pattern of planned arousal, to – in short – a technical theory of art.

Collingwood seems to sense this drift when he writes, 'An artist need not be a slave to a technical theory, in order to feel that his audience's approbation is relevant to the question whether he has done his work well or ill.' (313) Unless he sees the approval in the faces of his audience, 'he wonders whether he was speaking the truth or not.' (314) Collingwood is arguing here that artists and audiences collaborate in *judging* the work. This is not the same as their being collaborators in the aesthetic activity itself. He has shifted ground, perhaps to avoid endorsing a technical theory of art. And if artists see approval in the faces of their audiences, is that a sign that they have successfully expressed the mutual emotions? If they see instead incomprehension or outrage, is that a sign that they have failed artistically? Could it not be that they have annoyed complacency, baffled imperception, or hit on painful and unwelcome truth? One could immediately cite *Madame Bovary* or *Ulysses* among a host of examples of the ignorant or trivializing reception of major works of art. Collingwood's ground here seems radically unstable.

In section six of chapter fourteen, 'Aesthetic Individualism,' he attacks the romantic view of the artist as aesthetic superman and returns the argument to the view of the artist-audience relationship as a conversation among peers. Artists 'become poets or painters or musicians . . . by living in a society where these languages are current. . . . they speak to those who understand. . . . If he has a new emotion, he must express it to others, in order that, finding them able to share it, he may be sure that his consciousness is not corrupt.' (317) Such certainty is desirable, but does sharing guarantee it? 'The experience of being listened to . . . goes on in the mind of the speaker, although in order to [realize?][13] its existence a listener is necessary, so that the activity is a collaboration.' (317)

Section seven of chapter fourteen establishes the importance, the necessity even, of collaboration among artists, citing Shakespeare, Handel, Beethoven, Turner, Chartres cathedral, and the 1611 translation of the Bible. In section eight, he urges the necessity of close collaboration with performers by both composers and dramatists. 'Authors who try to produce a fool-proof text are choosing fools for their collaborators.' (321)

In the next section, 'The Artist and His Audience,' Collingwood, apparently wishing to carry the pattern of collaboration among artists and with performers to its conclusion, draws our attention to the oft-experienced impact of audiences in dramatic and concert performances. He compares the deadness of rehearsals in empty houses to the stimulating interplay with live audiences. It is, it should be noted however, the performers who are responding to the responsive audience, not the author or the composer. Nevertheless, Collingwood uses the performance arts as his model in the argument that follows. 'The printing press separates the author from his audience. . . .' (323) Likewise, in other arts that involve publication of some sort, 'the performers and the audience are out of touch.

The audience is not collaborating, it is only overhearing.' (PA 323). This statement will be further examined.

In the concluding chapter of *Principles* Collingwood sets forth various proposals for returning art to the communal, collaborative state that might restore its health. He urges the abandonment of copyright in order to stimulate emulation, borrowing, and competition among artists. For the performing arts he urges abandoning the heavy use of stage directions and musical expression marks since these discourage the necessary partnership between authors and actors, composers and musicians. He proposes the formation of communities of artists, performers, and sympathetic, demanding audiences, 'theatrical or musical clubs.' Such artistic communities are envisioned in considerable detail.

A major difficulty arises when he turns to 'the arts of publishing (notably painting and non-dramatic writing). . . . The promiscuous dissemination of books and paintings by the press and public exhibition creates a shapeless and anonymous audience whose collaborative function it is impossible to exploit.' He characterizes such audiences as 'this formless dust of humanity.' (330) This attitude has not been characteristic of Collingwood's thinking. Are we to oppose widespread, affordable publishing, increased literacy, and galleries and museums? '. . . there is a real likelihood that painting and non-dramatic literature may cease to exist. . . . Indeed, this has begun to happen already. The novel, once an important literary form, has all but disappeared, except as amusement for the semi-literate.' (330-31) To declare the demise of the novel at a time when Joyce, Lawrence, Woolf, Forster and Bowen were flourishing is bewildering. And when did unpublished novels have audiences?

He has forgotten, too, how his favorite novelist, Jane Austen, responded to something very like the proliferation of the amusement novel that he deplores. Fascinated and amused by the popular romances of her day, Austen in her teens parodies them, then invents a romance that deals with everyday events and problems in the lives of quite familiar sorts of people and so changes the history of the novel. And she was well received by her 'shapeless and anonymous audience,' some of them perhaps only semi-literate. Hers was a powerful artistic response to a felt audience appetite, and Collingwood stands among her most insightful and articulate admirers. For another counter-example, apparently Samuel Richardson's avid audience included illiterate people who gathered to hear *Pamela* read to them and rang churchbells when she finally married. The brilliant rise of the novel through the eighteenth and nineteenth centuries was surely fostered by the very leaps in publishing technology and literacy that, unaccountably, Collingwood now deplores.

A further counter-example from Collingwood's own writing: in 'Art,' a chapter from *Roman Britain and the English Settlements*,[14] he shows that the consumer art of Roman Britain was unable over several centuries to eradicate completely the powerful La Tène tradition of curvilinear Celtic art, a style which experienced a renaissance when the Romans left Britain.

This sidetracking by Collingwood from a most promising line of thought concludes with rather vague programmatic proposals. Authors should 'write on subjects which people want to read.' He doesn't mean 'subjects chosen for their power of arousing emotion,' for this, of course, would support a technical theory of amusement art. 'They are subjects about which people already have emotions, but confused and obscure ones. . . .' Such an author 'will have accepted the collaboration of his public from the very inception of his work. . . .' In such subject-matter 'lies the hope of a thriving literature yet to be written; for the subject-matter is the point at which the audience's collaboration can fertilize the writer's work.' (331-32) We are not told what such subjects might be, but a footnote refers us to Louis MacNeice's essay 'Subject in Modern Poetry.'[15] MacNeice argues that poetry should deal with the concerns of ordinary life (eschewing aestheticism) and praises Eliot and the later Yeats and, especially, Auden and Spender. This is perhaps the sort of subject Collingwood had in mind, for in his unpublished paper 'Aesthetic Theory and Artistic Practice' (1931)[16] he argued that both artists and philosophers try to clarify what their audience 'is already thinking and feeling obscurely.'

He concludes *Principles* with an insightful and enthusiastically admiring analysis of 'The Waste Land' (332-35) as the work of a poet who, 'laying aside his individualistic pretensions, walks as the spokesman of his audience.' The hopeful signs with which Collingwood prefaces this analysis have, however, another very discordant note. He speaks of painting and writing in 1937 as 'ceasing to rely on its amusement value to an audience of wealthy philistines, and . . . substituting for that aim not one of amusement value to an audience of wage-earners or dole-drawers . . .

but one of genuine artistic competence.' (333) Are these despised audiences borrowed from Eliot's poems?

'The Waste Land' inspires, at any rate, the last paragraph of *Principles,* which proposes an art of prophetic vision in which the artist 'tells his audience, at risk of their displeasure, the secrets of their own hearts. . . . Art is the community's medicine for the worst disease of mind, the corruption of consciousness.' (336)

Collingwood's characterization of audiences in these last few pages of *Principles* is perhaps a distorted echo of a brilliant essay he wrote a year earlier, 'Folklore and folk-tale.' In this essay he aims to break down conventional distinctions between folk art and 'fine art.'

> The folk-tale and the literary tale are . . . on the same footing. Each of them uses traditional themes and handles them by traditional methods; in each, the teller or writer modifies both the themes and the methods. . . . . . . each alike is simply a work of art: the supposed distinction between them turning out on analysis to be merely a distinction between two aspects – traditionality and originality, or receptiveness and creativeness – both of which are present in all works of art . . . [17]

Collingwood recalls in this essay the communal composition of the Bach family's 'Quodlibets' and the ease with which actors can improvise performances. Had he known enough, he might have cited the group improvisations of jazz. Detail by detail, elements of the final pages of *Principles* appear: borrowing among artists, judging audiences, creative intimacy between artist-performers and audiences, printing's disintegrating impact on the communal artistic community, the proliferation of stage directions and expression marks, the stultifying effect of notions of artistic individuality and ownership. All of these reappear, as we have seen, a year later in the more somber concluding pages of *Principles,* where such a communal world seems to Collingwood to have given way to a consumerist obsession with entertainment. It seems likely that the vision of folk art in this essay led to Collingwood's taking the audience interaction in the performing arts as models for the redemption of twentieth-century art.

Whether this be an explanation or not, his basic view of the artist-audience relationship, the view developed, as we have seen, through all but the last few pages of *Principles,* has staked out ground that can be profitably worked. The analysis of what imaginative reenactments by the audience entail and of the features of authors' texts which stimulate such reactions is the ground on which the reception aesthetic of Jauss and Iser has proved so fruitful.

The novelist who, Collingwood asserted, was able to 'lift in one hand all the mass of technical difficulties with which her predecessors had been struggling in vain . . . a village girl of twenty'[18] wrote on 29 January 1813 to inform her sister Cassandra that "I do not write for such dull elves' who have not a great deal of ingenuity themselves."[19] Wolfgang Iser has drawn attention to the explicit encouragement given by Fielding and Sterne to collaborative readers.[20]

> Bestir thyself; for though we will always lend thee proper assistance in difficult places, as we do not, like some others, expect thee to use the arts of divination to discover our meaning, yet we shall not indulge thy laziness where nothing but thy own attention is required; for thou art highly mistaken if thou dost imagine that we intended when we began this great work to leave thy sagacity nothing to do, or that without sometimes exercising this talent thou wilt be able to travel through our pages with any pleasure or profit to thyself. (*Tom Jones,* XI, 9, last paragraph)

> Writing, when properly managed, . . . is but a different name for conversation. . . . no author, who understands the just boundaries of decorum and good breeding, would presume to think all: The truest respect which you can pay to the reader's understanding, is to halve this matter amicably, and leave him something to imagine, in his turn . . .
>
> For my own part, I am eternally paying him compliments of this kind, and do all that lies in my power to keep his imagination as busy as my own. (*Tristram Shandy,* II, 11, first two paragraphs)

NOTES

1 (Oxford, Oxford University Press), 1924: 67.
2 (Oxford, Oxford University Press), 1925: 81-82.
3 Compare Hans Robert Jauss in 'Literary History as a Challenge to Literary Theory' for another statement of this idea. When the horizon shift imposed by major works has become the norm, when the works have thus become 'culinary' or entertainment art, reviving their artistic character 'requires a special effort to read them "against the grain".' *Toward an Aesthetic of Reception*, transl. Timothy Bahti (Minneapolis, University of Minnesota Press, 1982), 25-26.
4 Published in *The Hibbert Journal*, 24 (1926), 434-48. Quoted from the reprint in Collingwood's *Essays in the Philosophy of Art*, ed. Alan Donagan (Bloomington, University of Indiana Press, 1964), 196-97.
5 A series of lectures written in Die, France, and first published by W. J. van der Dussen in his new edition of Collingwood's *Idea of History* (Oxford, Oxford University Press, 1993). See, on re-enactment, 441-50.
6 That art is thought and that the artist's problem can, therefore, be imaginatively reenacted by the critic, the historian of art, the audience I have argued at length in section iv, Art and History, of 'R. G. Collingwood: Art, Craft, and History,' *Clio*, 2 (1973), 239-79. There I consider particularly Louis Mink's consideration of this problem in *Mind, History, and Dialectic: The Philosophy of R. G. Collingwood* (Bloomington and London, University of Indiana Press, 1969; rptd. Middletown, 1987), ch. 7.
7 First printed in *The Idea of History*, ed. T. M. Knox (Oxford, Oxford University Press, 1946), 282-302. Knox assembled this book from various manuscript and published sources after Collingwood's death. See W. J. van der Dussen's introduction to his 1993 edition for an account of Knox's sometimes regrettable editorial procedures. The pagination is identical in van der Dussen's edition.
8 See Jauss, *Toward an Aesthetic of Reception*, 29, and Iser, *the Act of Reading* (Baltimore and London, Johns Hopkins University Press, 1978) 73.
9 (Oxford, Oxford University Press, 1938), rptd. 1958.
10 See *The Implied Reader* (Baltimore and London, Johns Hopkins University Press, 1974), especially chapter eleven, and *The Act of Reading, passim* (see index).
11 Collingwood papers, Bodleian, folder 25.
12 Collingwood papers, Bodleian, folders 24 and 117.
13 Verb omitted at this point in the printed text.
14 (Oxford, Oxford University Press, 1936).
15 *Essays and Studies*, 22 (1937), 146-58.
16 Collingwood papers, Bodleian, folder 25, f.14.
17 Collingwood papers, Bodleian, folder 21, pp. 8-9
18 From the Austen lectures cited in note 11.
19 See *Jane Austen's Letters*, ed. R. W. Chapman (Oxford, Oxford University Press, 1952).
20 *The Implied Reader*, 31.

On Collingwood's Conceptions of History

GIUSEPPINA D'ORO
Keele University

Collingwood is probably one of the best known Anglo-American philosophers to have written on the nature of historical understanding. Yet, his major work on the nature of historical understanding, *The Idea of History*,[1] contains several accounts of history which appear to be non-coextensive. In this paper I consider three conceptions of history that co-exist within *The Idea of History*. I refer (somewhat arbitrarily and for lack of better labels) to these three conceptions of history as factual, formal and substantive. The first is to be found primarily in Collingwood's discussion of the historical imagination and the illustration of its workings in the section entitled 'Who killed John Doe?[2] The second is to be found in 'Human Nature and Human History'[3] but is also scattered throughout *The Idea of History*. I have referred to this second conception of history as formal, rather than factual, because on this view, history is not identified with something which occurred in the past and which is the task of the historian to discover; history is identified rather with a mode of explanation which is distinct from the kind of explanations that are given in natural science. It is this second conception of history that was, by and large, employed by W. H. Dray[4] in the attempt to defend Collingwood from Hempel's[5] claim that explanations in the natural sciences and in history have the same logical structure. It is also the conception of history that is usually appcalcd to in Collingwood-inspired discussions of the distinction between the understanding of actions and the explanation of events. I refer to the third conception of history to be found in *The Idea of History* as substantive. I have referred to this third conception of history as substantive rather than formal because it is concerned not only with the logical structure of historical explanation and the nature of the action/event distinction, but also with the nature of the fundamental beliefs that characterize historical periods and inform, whether explicitly or implicitly, the actions of historical agents. This conception of history is to be found in the second half of the Epilegomena.[6] This is probably the most neglected aspect of Collingwood's philosophy of history which is usually regarded as providing a model for the explanation of individual action rather than an attempt to understand the actions of individuals in the light of intersubjectively shared norms and principles.[7] My goal, in analysing these three conceptions of history, is neither to advance the claim that Collingwood's text is a patchwork of distinct, inconsistent and irreconcilable conceptions of history nor to question Knox's editorial work on the posthumously published manuscripts which have been included in *The Idea of History*, but rather to do a bit of conceptual housework.[8] It is also not my intention to make any claim for the exhaustiveness of the list I provide: the three conceptions of history discussed have been selected because they are pervasive and because they have been powerful enough to inspire different ways of approaching Collingwood's philosophy of history.

I

The first conception of history, I have claimed, is to be found in those passages in *The Idea of History*, which introduce the notion of the historical imagination and are illustrated in the detective work done on the case of John Doe. On this conception of history, the historian seeks to know something about events that occurred in the past. This conception of history is therefore factual because the knowledge that it seeks to obtain is empirical. On this conception of history the task of a philosophy of history is to explicate the method through which the past is known. As the historian does not have direct access to the events that he seeks to know (because these events occurred in the past) he attempts to reconstruct in his imagination what occurred in the past through a process of inference from something which he does know and which Collingwood calls evidence. Two important points ought to be made about Collingwood's account of evidence and of the historical imagination. First of all, nothing, for Collingwood can be regarded as evidence until it has passed through the critical judgement of historians. The statements of witnesses, for instance, are not, for the historian, authorities that ought not to be questioned. Rather whether a witness' report should or should not be regarded as evidence is something that ought to be determined by the historian. Collingwood makes this point by stating that the historian's activity is autonomous. Secondly, the historian's imaginative reconstruction of events, which he did not witness, is not arbitrary. It is through the historical imagination that it is possible to fill in the gaps of knowledge through a process of interpolation. Although the historian must reconstruct what happened in his imagination, this reconstruction is not subjective because it must be such as to take into account exhaustively the evidence: the conclusions which are reached through the process of interpolation are conclusions that anybody who has exhaustively examined the evidence available ought to reach. For this reason Collingwood likens the task of the historian to that of a detective and the workings of the historical imagination to the reconstruction of the scene of a crime in the detective's mind. History, understood in this way, as a reconstructive activity in which the historian has a high degree of autonomy in establishing what counts as evidence, is contrasted with the common sense conception of history where the relationship between the historian and the authority is that of the believer to the person believed (IH, 235). On the conception of history that Collingwood puts forward in 'The Historical Imagination', the role of the historian is to question rather than accept the statements of witnesses and it is in questioning the statements of witnesses that the historian manifests his autonomy. The historian's autonomy is manifested in the fact that the historian

> . . . has it in his power to reject something explicitly told him by his authorities and to substitute something else. If that is possible, the criterion of historical truth cannot be the fact that a statement is made by an authority. It is the truthfulness and the information of the so-called authority that are in question; and this question

the historian has to answer for himself, on his own authority. Even if he accepts what his authorities tell him, therefore, he accepts it not on their authority but on his own; not because they say it, but because it satisfies his criterion of historical truth' (IH, 237-38).

This conception of history is illustrated through the example of the detective work done on the case of John Doe's murder in which a) the testimony of the rector's daughter who confesses to the murder is discarded on the grounds that her motive was to protect her fiancé whom she (wrongly) suspects of having committed the crime and b) the real murderer (the rector) is uncovered by a combination of empirical evidence linking him to the scene of the crime (green paint from John Doe's recently varnished gate on the rector's jacket and gloves) and psychological work establishing his motives. It is important to point out that although this conception of history is factual or empirical in the sense that the goal of the historian is to find out certain facts about the past, the criterion of historical truth is not. The historian's account is said to be true to the extent that the hypothesis advanced fits the evidence beyond any reasonable doubt: the criterion of historical truth is that of narrative coherence. What makes the historian's account of the past true is not its correspondence with the facts (facts that the historian is not able to witness) but its ability to convince, with the degree of persuasiveness that the hero of a detective novel, who has exhaustively examined the possibilities and cross-examined the witnesses, exercises on the reader. Collingwood concedes that this criterion of historical truth does not deliver knowledge that is completely final as, in imaginatively reconstructing the past, the historian relies on the evidence available to him at the time and on the technical expertise of the day (IH, 248). On this conception of history historical knowledge is both compelling and subject to revision.

II

I would now like to turn to a second conception of history to be found in Collingwood's writings. According to this, the subject matter of history is actions rather than events and historical explanations are identified with explanations that are suitable to describe the former rather than the latter. Historical explanations are therefore identified with teleological/ purposive explanations and are contrasted with mechanistic ones. This conception of history is to be found both in chapter XXIX of *An Essay on Metaphysics* and in various places in *The Idea of History*. In chapter XXIX of *An Essay on Metaphysics*,[9] Collingwood lists three types of causes or explanatory principles in a discussion that is reminiscent of Aristotle's account of the four causes in his own *Metaphysics* and *Physics*. The term cause, Collingwood says, is employed in what he refers to as sense I, in the historical sciences where 'that which is caused is the free and deliberate act of a conscious and responsible agent, and causing him to do it means affording him a motive for so doing' (EM, 285). The term cause in sense I is made up of two elements, the *causa quod* and the *causa ut*. The *causa ut* is a purpose. The *causa quod* is not an antecedent condition but the agent's perception of the situation of action, that is, not an antecedent state of affairs, but an antecedent state of affairs known or believed by an agent to exist. Secondly, the term cause is employed in sense II in the practical sciences of nature, such as medicine and engineering where 'that which is caused is an event in nature and its cause is an event or state of things by producing or preventing which we can produce or prevent that whose cause is said to be' (EM, 296-97). Finally the term cause is discussed in sense III in the theoretical sciences of nature, such as physics, where 'that which is caused is an event or state of things and its cause is another event or state of things such that (a) if the cause happens or exists the effect must happen or exist even if not further conditions are fulfilled and (b) the effect cannot happen or exist unless the cause happens or exists'. Collingwood's discussion of the three senses of the term cause is more complex than it transpires from this brief exposition but the main points to be noted for the purpose of the present discussion are two.[10] The first is that explanations vary in accordance with context and that an explanation that is perfectly appropriate in one context may be inappropriate in another. To use one of Collingwood's own examples: it would be inappropriate, for an AA man to reason as a physicist rather than a mechanic and to explain to the driver of a car parked on the side of a road that the car failed to climb up the steep hill because 'the top of the hill is farther away from the earth's center than its bottom and consequently more power is needed to take the car uphill than to take her along the level' (EM, 302-3). One would rather expect the AA man to open the bonnet, find a loose high-tension cable and explain that the car could not climb up the hill because the car was running on three cylinders only (EM, 302-3). The second important point that emerges from Collingwood's discussion of the three causes is that whereas naturalistic explanations, whether in the practical or in the theoretical sciences of nature, are concerned with the relationship holding between states of affairs, explanations in the historical sciences are concerned with the relationship holding between purposes and beliefs on the one hand, and actions on the other. Although, to my knowledge, Collingwood never explicitly connected the account of historical causation given in *An Essay on Metaphysics* with his account of the action/ event distinction in *The Idea of History*, Collingwood's discussion of the term cause as it is employed in the historical sciences, underpins his claim, in *The Idea of History*, that the subject matter of history is actions, not events, and that actions differ from events because they have an inside or thought side that events lack. In *The Idea of History* Collingwood develops an extended argument aimed at showing that the employment of explanatory principles, which are perfectly appropriate within the context of natural science, to the domain of human affairs, results in explanations that are inappropriately naturalistic. The task of the historian, Collingwood claims, is not to formulate empirical laws on the basis of observed regularities of behaviour, but to reconstruct a practical argument or syllogism in which the deliberation to act is the conclusion and the agent's assessment of the situation in which he has to act and his motives are the epistemic and motivational premises. Historical explanations, therefore, seek to establish a logical link between the premises and the conclusions of an argument, not an external or empirical connection between the occurrence of a bodily movement and its antecedent conditions. In this respect historical explanations are more akin to common sense explanations for human behaviour than they are to scientific hypotheses. What we do when we explain human behaviour within the framework of vernacular psychology is to analyse how individuals respond to certain situations by drawing inferences from a number of premises and act on the conclusion of an argument that the folk-psychologist reconstructs on the agent's behalf. For instance, if, as a folk-psychologist, I attempted to explain why a Mr. Jones declined an employment offer for an high powered managerial position with a firm by saying that Jones declined the job offer because the firm operates a policy of employing illegal immigrants in order to cut production costs, what I am likely to mean is that Jones had reasons, be these of an ethical or legal nature, for declining the offer: 'Jones declined the job offer because the company operates a particular employment policy' is a short-hand explanation for 'Jones declined the offer because he objects, on moral/legal grounds, to the company's employment policy'. The long, as opposed to the short-hand version of the explanation makes it clear that the motivations for the act is sought in an agent's response to a particular situation, rather than the situation itself. Unlike scientific hypotheses, common-sense explanations of this kind are not attempts at explaining the behaviour of agents by appealing to empirical regularities: when, as a folk-psychologist, I attempt to explain Jones' behaviour, I am unlikely to ask myself the question 'what are the conditions which usually precede the rejection of employment offers?' a question that would be structurally analogous to the one that, for Collingwood, is asked by the empirical scientist: 'on what kind of occasions do pieces of litmus turn pink?' Historians, like folk-psychologists, do not regard the behaviour of historical agents as knee-jerk reactions to antecedent conditions but as intelligent responses mediated by consciousness and will. This is why historical explanations are explanations of actions. This second conception of history may be referred as formal because it focuses on the logical structure of historical explanations. It is this conception of history that informs Collingwood-inspired discussions of the distinction between explanation in the social and in the natural sciences which have been employed by philosophers such as Dray to undermine any attempt to obliterate the distinction and to deny the autonomy of history.

This account of historical explanation, according to which explanations in history are, to use a term coined by Dray, 'rational' explanations,[11] was often subjected to a certain standard criticism. It was claimed that the model of explanation which Collingwood wished to adopt and according to which actions are the expression of a valid practical argument is inadequate because human beings are not fully rational and consequently may fail to see what conclusions follow from which premises. The objection that Collingwood neglects that many human actions are not rational, but random, and consequently, that he endorses an overly intellectualistic account of action, seems to be premised on a misunderstanding of the nature of the enterprise in which Collingwood was engaging in *The Idea of History*. *The Idea of History* is concerned with the concept of action, not with particular human actions and it consequently describes actions, as they ought to be, i.e., as expressions of thought. As the moral philosopher engaged in the project of describing and expounding the concept of the right abstracts from the way in which individuals at times act, i.e., wrongly or immorally, the philosopher engaged in describing and expounding the concept of action must likewise abstract from the way in which individuals at times act, that is, irrationally, randomly or unthinkingly. As nobody, in their right mind, would object to the moral philosopher engaged in the project of clarifying what is the concept of the right, by pointing out that people do not always act morally, nobody, in their right mind, should object to the project of expounding the concept of action by pointing out that not all human doings are actions. Objections of this type will always arise as long as one fails to understand the nature of Collingwood's enterprise in *The Idea of History*. Whereas Collingwood is certainly concerned with the activities of practising historians and a reflection on their activities provides a starting point for his enquiry, *The Idea of History* can hardly be regarded as the work of a practising historian or as an applied historiography. Practising historians are concerned with particular actions which may or may not be rational. Collingwood, on the other hand, rarely focuses on specific historical events and his occasional references to particular historical agents are too sketchy to be taken as examples of historical explanations. It is therefore necessary to distinguish between the concerns of practising historians or of an applied historiography and Collingwood's concern in *The Idea of History*. Practising historians are concerned with particular actions whereas *The Idea of History* is concerned with the concept of action. Undoubtedly, in order to elucidate the concept of action as such, Collingwood has to resort to particular actions, such as those of Caesar or Brutus, but this ought not to suggest that his claims are made at the level of an applied historiography. Therefore, even Collingwood's occasional references to particular actions are best understood not as examples borrowed from historical practice but rather as illustrations of a basic conceptual distinction.[12]

This conception of history differs from the previous one in several important respects. First, history in this sense, is not concerned with factual knowledge, but with the thoughts of historical agents: if the subject matter of history is actions, rather than events, and action-oriented explanations establish internal or logical, i.e., non empirical connections between the *explanans* (the epistemic and motivational premises) and the *explanandum* (the action), historical knowledge is not factual in nature. Secondly, this conception of history differs from the previous one because its object is not the past but mind. Given that history does not study mere behaviour or bodily movements but actions and that actions are expression of thought, what makes understanding historical is not the fact that it studies the past but that it studies mind. Thirdly, when this conception of history prevails over the first one, Collingwood's emphasis appears to be not so much on the historian's autonomy vis-à-vis the statements of witnesses, but with the autonomy of history as a discipline with a distinct method and domain of enquiry from that of the natural sciences. On this second conception of history the autonomy of history thesis is not a thesis about the critical powers of historians but about the emancipation of history from the tutelage of natural science.[13] Fourthly, whereas in both cases Collingwood claims that historical inference is not inductive in nature, the denial that history is an inductive science appears to be motivated by different agendas. In his account of the historical imagination Collingwood seems to deny that historical inference is inductive on the grounds that the conclusions reached by historians are as compelling as those reached by the hero of a detective novel whereas inductive inferences never have that kind of argumentative force; on the other hand, when contrasting the notion of historical causation with that of natural causation, Collingwood seems to deny that historical explanations are inductive, not because the conclusions reached by historians are compelling, but because historical explanations, unlike explanations in the natural sciences seek to bring to light an internal or logical connection between motives/beliefs and actions, rather than an external or empirical connection between state of affairs. Finally, whereas in his account of the historical imagination Collingwood searches for a criterion for historical truth (even if, granted, not one which is based on the correspondence theory of knowledge) in his account of the action/event distinction what matters is not truth but appropriateness to the context of explanation.

III

I would now like to turn to consider a third conception of history to be found in Collingwood's writings. I will refer to this third conception of history as substantive to distinguish it from what I referred to as a formal conception of history or a conception of history that is primarily concerned with the structure of the explanation. On this third conception of history the object of history is what Collingwood occasionally refers to as the corporate mind of an age and a philosophy of history of this kind seeks to understand what are the intersubjectively shared norms and beliefs that inform the actions of historical agents. On this conception of history the role of a philosophy of history is neither that of articulating a method for the acquisition of knowledge about past events (as in the first conception of history) nor is it that of articulating the structure of historical explanation (as in the second) but to study those fundamental principles and beliefs which constitute the unity of historical periods and in the light of which the actions of individuals may be understood. This conception of history is to be found, for instance, in the first section of the Epilegomena (§ I Human Nature and Human History, (i) The Science of Human Nature, IH, 205 ff.) and it is articulated in an attempt to answer the question 'why do historians habitually identify history with the history of human affairs?' (IH, 213). In an attempt to answer this question Collingwood says that whereas it is indeed the case that historians are usually concerned with phenomena of a social or political nature (such as battles and conquests), rather than with natural phenomena (such as earthquakes, volcanic explosions, flooding and the likes) it would be mistaken to reply, in answer to the question just posed, that historians focus on the domain of human affairs because they are concerned with human actions. Having rejected a straightforward identification of the subject matter of history (the domain of human affairs), with human actions, Collingwood proceeds to explain the distinction between historical and non-historical action as follows:

> It does not follow that all human actions are subject matter for history; and indeed historians are agreed that they are not. But when they are asked how the distinction is to be made between historical

and non-historical human actions, they are somewhat at a loss to reply. From our present point of view we can offer an answer: so far as a man's conduct is determined by what may be called his animal nature, his impulses and appetites, it is non-historical; the process of those activities is a natural process. Thus the historian is not interested in the fact that men, eat and sleep, and make love and thus satisfy their natural appetites; but he is interested in the social customs they create by their thought as a framework within which these appetites find satisfaction (IH, 216).

This way of identifying the subject matter of history, via a justification of the distinction between historical and non-historical human actions, makes it clear that, according to Collingwood, history studies thought or mind not, or not only, in the sense that it studies intelligent responses as opposed to knee-jerk reactions, but in the sense that it is concerned with the social dimension of human actions, with 'social customs . . . as a framework in which . . . appetites find satisfaction'. Hence history is concerned with rational rather than natural processes not simply in the sense that it studies thoughtful rather than thoughtless or mechanical responses but primarily in the sense that it is concerned with those intersubjectively valid norms, be these epistemic, moral or aesthetic, which structure the lives of individuals as members of organised communities. Where there is no culture or civilization, Collingwood claims, there can be no history and consequently there can be no such thing as a history of mankind's state of nature or indeed of any state of nature, such as a history of the animal kingdom.[14] As Collingwood puts it in *The Principles of History*:[15]

> . . . a great many things which deeply concern human beings are not, and never have been, traditionally included in the subject-matter of history. People are born, eat and breathe and sleep, and beget children and become ill and recover again, and die; and these things interest them, most of them at any rate, far more than art and science, industry and politics and war. Yet none of these things have been traditionally regarded as possessing historical interest. Most of them have given rise to institutions like dining and marrying

and the various rituals that surround birth and death, sickness and recovery; and of these rituals and institutions people write histories; but the history of dining is not the history of eating, and the history of death-rituals is not the history of death (PH, 46).

On this (third) conception of history the subject matter of history is mind, understood not so much as the thoughts of individual agents but as the corporate mind of an age and the task of understanding the past is equivalent to understanding habits of mind that are no longer shared by the historian.

An important feature of this third conception of history is that it conceives of the idea or concept of history as being logically prior to the idea of nature. The thesis concerning the logical priority of the idea of history over the idea of nature is expressed in *The Principles of History* where Collingwood states that from the perspective of a philosophy of history there can be no such thing as nature in-itself:

> The thesis I have undertaken to defend is that no historian can ever find 'nature as it actually and indefeasibly is', or 'nature in itself', among the factors that influence the course of history. What influences the course of history is not nature in itself, but the beliefs about nature, true or false, entertained by the human beings whose actions are in question. It was not the eclipse, but his belief that days with eclipses on them were unlucky, that influenced so disastrously Nicia's siege of Syracuse. It is not the fact that typhoid is endemic there, but our belief that it is, combined with our belief in a certain method of prophylaxis, that influences us to inoculate our troops when they are going to operate there (PH, 96-97).

The idea or concept of history is said to be logically prior to the idea or concept of nature because, what nature is, depends on the historical articulation of reality, which includes a people's conception of nature: there is, strictly speaking, no such thing as knowledge of nature in-itself, there can be only knowledge of nature for us. In other words, the idea of nature too is part of the historical articulation of reality, of the history of thought:

> What man, at any stage of history, thinks of himself as dealing with, when we say he is dealing with nature, is never nature as it is in-itself but always nature as at that stage of history he conceives it. All history is the history of thought: and wherever in history anything called nature appears, either this name stands not for nature in itself but for man's thought about nature, or else history has forgotten that it has come of age, and has fallen back into its old state of pupilage to natural science (PH, 98).

As, on this third or substantive conception of history, the idea of history is conceived to be logically prior to the idea of nature, history carries the weight of Collingwood's idealism[16] or of his anti-realist metaphysics. This is so because whereas the historian, if he is to understand the statements of historical agents, must set aside any notion of reality as it might be in itself and focus on the historical agents' conception of reality, the natural scientist, if he is to investigate nature, must claim to investigate reality in itself, independently of the agents' conceptualization of it and, therefore, as if it had no history. Hence whereas historical enquiry is an expression of Collingwood's anti-realism, the practice of natural science is the expression of the very realism that constituted the target of Collingwood's life-long philosophical project.

The third conception of history is arguably the least explored of Collingwood's three conceptions of history. Its relative neglect is due to a number of reasons. First, the discussion of Collingwood's philosophy of history within so-called analytical philosophy of history has tended to focus on purely formal or methodological issues. Walsh's distinction between critical and speculative philosophy of history is, to some extent, an expression of the separation of formal from substantive issues in analytical philosophy of history.[17] According to Walsh there are two kinds of philosophers of history: those who are concerned with formal questions, such as the nature of historical explanation, and those who are concerned with questions surrounding the goal, purpose or meaning of history. Collingwood is said to belong to the first group and to practise critical history, whereas philosophers such as Hegel are said to be speculative philosophers of history. The distinction is not helpful because it tends to falsify Collingwood's concept of history. In fact, whereas it is indubitably true that Collingwood is not a speculative philosopher of history (he does not have a grand-narrative of historical development especially if this grand-narrative is understood as a prospective teleology), his conception of history as a rational process is much closer to the Hegelian notion of 'philosophical history' than many have cared to admit. Some aspects of Collingwood's critique of scissors-and-paste history, for instance, bear quite striking similarities to Hegel's critique of reflective history in the introduction to his *Lectures on the Philosophy of World History*.[18] Another reason for the relative neglect of this third conception of history may be sought in the fact that traditionally Collingwood's notion of historical understanding has been construed in individualistic terms and the task of the historian has been seen as that of reconstructing the thought processes that for instance, a general might have gone through in preparation for a battle rather than attempt to understand the actions of individuals in relationship to certain intersubjective norms, be these epistemic, moral or legal. The tendency to interpret Collingwood's philosophy of history in individualistic terms has prevailed in spite of the fact that Collingwood's most cited illustration of the action/event distinction seems to suggest that by the inside or thought-side of action is meant not so much the thought process of an individual but the meaning or significance that the action has in its contemporary setting:

> The historian, investigating any event in the past, makes a distinction between what may be called the outside and the inside of an event. By the outside of the event I mean everything belonging to it which can be described in terms of bodies and their movements: the passage of Caesar, accompanied by certain men, across a river called the Rubicon at one date, or the spilling of his blood on the floor of the senate-house at another. By the inside of the event I mean that in it which can only be described in terms of thought: Caesar's defiance of Republican law, or the clash of constitutional policy between himself and his assassins. The historian . . . is interested in the crossing of the Rubicon only in its relation to Republican law, and in the spilling of Caesar's blood only in its relation to a constitutional conflict (IH, 213).

The resilience of the claim that Collingwood's philosophy of history is concerned primarily with the understanding of individual action rather than attempt to understand the actions of individuals in the light of certain intersubjectively valid norms, may be due to the fact that often, those who appealed to Collingwood in the attempt to defend the autonomy of history thesis against Hempel's onslaught, denied the reducibility of historical explanations to explanations in the natural sciences by stating that whereas explanations in the natural sciences are nomological, explanations in history are not: if the actions of individuals were explained by subsuming them under a general law, they would be treated in a way that is more appropriate to natural objects or events.[19] Whereas this observation is, in one sense, correct, because Collingwood did not believe the purpose of historical enquiry to be that of either predicting or retrodicting human behaviour, it is important to point out that Collingwood did not reject completely the idea of nomologicality in history. There is, for Collingwood, such a thing as typical behaviour or behaviour that characterizes the action of certain historical individuals in a given historical period. What Collingwood rejects, is not the idea that there can be regularities of behaviour, but that such regularities should be explained on the basis of a method, that of observation and inductive generalisation, that is appropriate only for the investigation of an unchanging subject matter. As Collingwood puts it:

> Types of behaviour no doubt, recur, so long as minds of the same kind are placed in the same kinds of situations. The behaviour-patterns characteristic of a feudal baron were no doubt fairly constant so long as there were feudal barons living in a feudal society. But they will be sought in vain (except by an enquirer content with the loosest and most fanciful analogies) in a world whose social structure is of another kind . . . a positive science of mind will, no doubt, be able to establish uniformities and recurrences, but it can have no guarantee that the laws it establishes will hold good beyond the historical period from which its facts are drawn (IH, 223-4).

Collingwood did not reject the idea of generalisations in history; what he denied is that such generalisations can be arrived at inductively by observing regularities of behaviour. Since history is concerned with actions, and actions are more than mere behaviour or bodily movements, actions of the same kind can occur only when there are minds of the same kind. The concept of nomologicality in history is captured, therefore, not by the notion of an empirical generalisation but by the idea of a period, which is described as a unity of principles or ideas:

> ... when we isolate a period in history for study, we do so in virtue of a unity or homogeneity which we see it to possess. Since all history is the history of thought, this unity is a unity of thought – a unity in the thought of the persons whose actions form our period. That is to say, it is a unity of principles or ideals (Outlines of a Philosophy of History, in IH, 479).

The reason why empirical generalisations are of little help to the historian is not because actions are so unique as to be unclassifiable, but because in order for generalisations about actions to be appropriately carried out one must take into account the inter-subjectively valid moral legal and epistemic norms which inform the behaviour of historical agents. In sum: on this conception of history the subject matter of history is mind, understood not so much as the thoughts of individual agents but as the corporate mind and the task of understanding the past is equivalent to understanding habits of mind that are no-longer shared by the historian.[20]

This third or substantive conception of history differs from the second at least in the following important respects. First, Collingwood tends to focus on certain habits of mind or fundamental principles which are characteristic of historical periods rather than discuss the mere concept of action. Secondly, to the extent that, on this conception of history, Collingwood's thought is on the corporate mind, rationality is identified not merely with logical validity but with the nature of those fundamental historical principles from which inferences are drawn, principles may be so fundamental and so unquestioned as to function as to have the status of suppressed premises. Thirdly, instead of arguing for the autonomy of history from natural science Collingwood's tends to argue for what seems to be a rather stronger thesis: the logical priority of the idea of history over the idea of nature. Whereas the autonomy of history thesis entails only that from an historical point of view one must describe human action as expressions of thought, in the way in which, from the point of view of a science of nature, one must regard human actions on a par with any other empirically classifiable event, the thesis of the logical priority of the idea of history over the idea of nature seems to entail the stronger claim that every point of view, is, in the last analysis, historical. Hence Collingwood's claim that there cannot be any such thing as a philosophy of nature understood as the study of the ultimate structure of reality as opposed to the study of how the notion of nature has been historically articulated. Finally, whereas on the second conception of history, history is a form of experience alongside others such as religion, art natural science etc., on the third conception of history the historian looks at conceptions of religion, of art and of natural science prevalent in any given historical period.[21]

It is in defence of this conception of history, or better, of its possibility that, I believe, Collingwood developed his account of re-enactment. The term re-enactment is probably one of the most controversial terms and indeed concepts in Collingwood's philosophy of history. In the early days of Collingwood scholarship the re-enactment doctrine was criticized by the likes of Gardiner for its Cartesian overtones[22] and Collingwood was accused of reviving what Ryle had exposed as the myth of the ghost in the machine. These objections were later overcome mainly through the interpretative efforts of Dray whose work attempted to show that terms such as 'the inside/thought-side of action' were metaphorical ways of expressing the view that explanations in history have a different logical structure from explanations in the natural sciences. The term re-enactment, however, tends to be used by Collingwood in a very specific context, i.e., in the context of the claim that the thoughts of historical agents are not in principle unknowable because thought or mind, unlike empirical facts and events stands outside of time. In other words, whereas the term re-enactive explanation is often used to refer to Collingwood's claim that explanations in history have a different logical structure from explanations in the natural sciences, the context of Collingwood's discussion of the re-enactment doctrine is the attempt to show that the past is not in principle unknowable, that it is possible for historians to re-enact or rethink the thoughts of historical agents.[23] Collingwood's account of re-enactment is very much concerned with the question of principle, rather than that of fact: he readily admits, for instance that there are historical periods which are obscure or unknown, such as the middle ages and explains that their being obscure is due to the fact that the historian is incapable of recovering the habits of mind characteristic of that period:

> It may thus be said that historical enquiry reveals to the historian the powers of his own mind. Since all he can know historically is thoughts he can re-think for himself, the fact of his coming to know them shows him that his mind is able . . . to think in these ways. And conversely, whenever he finds certain historical matters unintelligible, he has discovered a limitation of his own mind; he has discovered that there are certain ways in which he is not, or no longer, or not yet, able to think. Certain historians, sometimes whole generations of historians, find in certain periods of history nothing intelligible, and call them dark ages; but such phrases tell us nothing about those ages themselves, though they tell us a great deal about the persons who use them, namely that they are unable to rethink the thoughts which were fundamental to their life (IH, 218-9).

Much of Collingwood's account of re-enactment in *The Idea of History* consists in a discussion of a certain thesis in the philosophy of mind that would make not only the thought of historical agents, but also those of any other agent, in principle unknowable. The thesis, which is attributed to an imaginary objector, identifies thought with psychological processes or token acts of thinking and, Collingwood argues, is, as a result, unable to account for how two agents may share the same thought. If thought is identified with token acts, the criteria of identity of thought are numerical; yet, if numerical criteria of identity are employed, no two psychological acts can be said to be (numerically) the same and by implication, no two agents can be said to have or share the same thought. Collingwood's reply to the position in the philosophy of mind exemplified by the imaginary objector is to state that it is a mistake to identify thought with token psychological acts because thought, unlike the acts in which it is exemplified, stands outside of time. According to Collingwood, whereas token acts of thinking can be ascribed spatial and temporal properties (it makes sense to ask when/where questions about them) it does not make sense to ask of the content of thought when or where it occurs. Whereas token psychological acts have duration and location, thought does not: we can ask of a thought-content whether it is interesting or boring, cogent, valid or invalid, not how long it lasts and where it is. It in this sense that thought, as opposed to token acts of thinking, is said to 'stand outside of time'. Historians, according to Collingwood, can rethink the same thoughts of historical agents because thoughts are identified by reference neither to their duration or location, but their content. Although Collingwood's discussion of re-enactment is carried out at a certain level of abstraction in so far as it deals with a position in the philosophy of mind that appears to be rather remote from the concerns of a philosophy of history, it does have clear implications for Collingwood's notion of historical understanding: to the extent that historians can immerse themselves in past habits of mind, they can be said to have knowledge of the past; the past is not in principle unknowable.

IV

In this last section I would like to provide some reflections on the relationship in which the three conceptions of history just outlined stand to one another. My view on this is that whereas the second and the third conceptions of history do not presuppose radically different notions of historical understanding, the first conception of history presupposes a very different account of historical understanding and of its object. Whereas the second and third conceptions of history are both concerned with the question as to how is historical understanding possible (and understanding is said to be historical if its object is mind), the first conception of history seems to have been developed in the attempt to answer the question as to how knowledge of past events, i.e., events not accessible to observation, is possible (the defining characteristic of historical knowledge is not that it studies mind but that it studies what cannot be observed because past). There are important differences between the second and third conception of history although such differences are not so radical as to entail different account of the domain of enquiry of history. As we have already seen the third conception of history introduces substantive considerations which are not taken into account in the second, whose main concern is to lay bare the logical structure of mentalistic explanations as opposed to looking at historical periods as the expression of a rational process in which the actions of individuals are understood against the background of the development of civilization. Further it is to the extent that Collingwood introduces substantive considerations that the notion of historical action is contrasted not so much with behaviour which is arbitrary or irrational but with behaviour which is non-rational in the sense that it belongs to the natural rather than historical condition of mankind. Nonetheless, although there are important differences between the second or formal and the third or substantive conception of history, these conceptions of history are like two sides of the same coin. The formal conception of history studies the logical structure of historical explanation or lays bare the nature of historical inference; the third or substantive conception of history looks at this structure in a concrete context. Both, however, present history as a study of mind or thought. In fact, the distinction between the second and third conception of history, like that between analytical and substantive philosophy of histories, may be more a feature of Collingwood scholarship than of Collingwood's own thought as he repeatedly claimed that historical explanations apply indifferently to the individual and to the collective mind implying, consequently, that there is no constraint to applying the basic model of historical inference to the study of collective thought.[24] Whereas the second and third conceptions of history do not work with radically different notions of historical understanding, the first conception of history appears to be formulated in answer to different questions: in the sections on the historical imagination Collingwood is concerned primarily with the issue of how events not available to observation can be known and his critique of scissors-and-paste history appears to be motivated by the attempt to establish the historian's right never to take the statements of witnesses as true rather than by the attempt to establish what is the appropriate way of studying the mind. Collingwood, in other words, is not, in this context, pursuing the rather different project of demonstrating that the historian who attempts to understand the statements of witnesses from the perspective of his own conceptual framework (as in the instance of the devil fearer) will fail to understand them and produce, as a result, ahistorical, naturalistic explanations. The nature of historical inference, as described in the passages on the historical imagination and the detective work on the case of John Doe, differs quite radically from the nature of historical inference as described in *An Essay on Metaphysics* and in those passages in *The Idea of History* concerned with the nature of the action/event distinction. The discussion of the action/event distinction in *The Idea of History* and of the nature of historical causation in *An Essay on Metaphysics*, suggest that historical inference uncovers logical or internal relations between the premises and conclusions of a practical argument whereas in the passage on John Doe inference proceeds from something known, the evidence, to the reconstruction of the unobserved. On the basis of these considerations we may say that there are two rather fundamental differences between the first conception of history and the other two. First, whereas the second and third conceptions of history provide criteria for historical understanding, the first conception of history provides a criterion for historical truth. Secondly, whereas the concept of history as the study of mind entails that the domain of enquiry of history is what may be referred to as 'the space of reasons', the concept of history as the study of events that are not available to observation (because they are past/rather than because they are rational processes), entails that the domain of enquiry of history is factual and gives rise to a philosophy of history with a much stronger empirical content.

As mentioned at the beginning, the purpose of this paper is neither to claim that *The Idea of History* is a patchwork of different and not easily reconcilable claims concerning the nature of history and historical enquiry, nor to question the editorial work done by Knox, but purely to put the house in order. Whereas Knox's editorial work may have distorted the reception of Collingwood.[25] The presence of different conceptions of history may have deeper roots: it may ultimately have to be explained by Collingwood's dual personality as an historian with an interest in history as an academic discipline practiced in history departments and as a philosopher with an interest in the concept of history as a vehicle for articulating the thesis of the logical priority of practical over theoretical reason.

NOTES

1 R. G. Collingwood, *The Idea of History* (Oxford, Oxford University Press, 1994), edited with an introduction by Jan van der Dussen.
2 This I believe, has inspired the work of, amongst others, L. Pompa 'Truth and Fact in History', in *Substance and Form in History*, edited by L. Pompa and W. H. Dray (Edinburgh, Edinburgh University Press, 1981); L. B. Cebick, 'Collingwood: Action, Re-enactment and Evidence', *Philosophical Forum*, 2 (1970); L. J. Goldstein, *Historical Knowing* (Austin, University of Texas Press, 1976) and 'History and the Primacy of Knowing', *History and Theory* 16 (1977).
3 IH, part V, Epilegomena, § I.
4 See for instance, 'Historical Understanding as Rethinking', *University of Toronto Quarterly* 27, (1957); 'R. G. Collingwood and the Understanding of Actions in History' in W. H. Dray, *Perspectives on History* (Routledge and Kegan Paul, London, 1980).
5 C. Hempel, 'The Function of General Laws in History', *Journal of Philosophy* 39 (1942).
6 IH, section V, 'History as re-enactment of past experience', 'The Subject Matter of History' and 'History and Freedom'.
7 The notion of a substantive notion of history in Collingwood is discussed by Bruce Haddock in 'Vico, Collingwood and the Character of a Historical Philosophy', and by Jan van der Dussen in 'Collingwood and the Idea of Process, Progress and Civilization', both in *Philosophy, History and Civilization: Interdisciplinary Perspectives on R. G. Collingwood*, edited by David Boucher, James Connelly and Tariq Modood (Cardiff, University of Wales Press, 1995).
8 For an account of Knox's editorial work on *The Idea of History* and the unedited material see D. Boucher's 'The Significance of Collingwood's Principles of History', *Journal of the History of Ideas* 58, 1997 and Jan van der Dussen, 'Collingwood's 'Lost' Manuscript of *The Principles of History*', *History and Theory* 36 (1997).
9 R. G. Collingwood, *An Essay on Metaphysics* (Oxford, Oxford University Press, 1940).
10 For an account of the three senses of the term cause see W. H. Dray, 'Historical Causation and Human Free Will', *University of Toronto Quarterly* 29 (1960) and R. Martin, 'Collingwood on Reasons, Causes and the Explanation of Action' in *International Studies in Philosophy* (1991), 23.
11 W. H. Dray, 'The Historical Explanation of Actions Reconsidered' in S. Hook (ed) *Philosophy and History* (New York, New York University Press, 1963).
12 It may be argued, for instance, that Collingwood's *The Idea of History* stands to an applied historiography as Kant's *Groundwork for a Metaphysics of Morals* stands to an applied ethics. In the way in which in Kant's Groundwork, the descriptions of the shopkeeper who returns the correct change in order to retain his custom and of the man who helps others in distress despite having lost any feeling for his fellow human beings, are put forward as illustrations of the distinction between 'acting in accordance' with duty and 'acting out' of duty, rather than as concrete examples of instrumental and moral actions, Collingwood references to Caesar are illustrations of the conceptual distinction between actions and events, they are not put forward as explanations for what Caesar did, that is, as examples of historical explanations.
13 Collingwood's heroes also seem to shift from Bacon (whose example, Collingwood says, the historian should follow in putting not nature but the testimony of witnesses, to the torture), and to Vico (who first understood that the question the historian should pose is not whether the statements contained in historical sources are true or false but what they mean).

14 Collingwood denies that there can be a history of the animal kingdom because, to the extent that non-human animals have no civilization, they live in a perpetual state of nature: their condition is natural not because they are not human but because, unlike humans, they have no civilization and cannot, therefore, have a history.

15 *The Principles of History and Other Writings in Philosophy of History*, edited with an introduction by W. H. Dray and W. J. van der Dussen (Oxford, Oxford University Press, 1999).

16 Collingwood denied being an idealist partly because he did not want his form of anti-realism to be identified either with the ontological or metaphysical idealism of Berkeley nor with the psychological or subjective idealism of which Hegel accused Kant. With the proviso that his form of anti-realism is neither ontological (denies the existence of an external world) nor psychological (makes claims about psychological processes that lead to the acquisition of knowledge rather than about the logical conditions of knowledge), he may be referred to as an idealist.

17 W. H. Walsh, *An Introduction to the Philosophy of History* (London, Hutchingson University Press, 1967).

18 Hegel's critique of reflective history, in a nutshell, consists in claiming that the reflective historian looks at the past whilst using the conceptual framework of the present, thereby failing to understand the past historically. This is exactly what prompts Collingwood to critique the historiographical principles which lie at the basis of Hume's treatment of miracles in the *Inquiries* and of Bradley's account of mesmeric events in *The Presuppositions of Critical History* in the famous example of the devil fearer:

> If the reasons why it is hard for a man to cross the mountains is because he is frightened of the devils in them, it is folly for the historian, preaching at him across a gulf of centuries, to say 'This is sheer superstition. There are no devils at all. Face facts, and realise that there are no dangers in the mountains except rocks and water and snow, wolves perhaps, and bad men perhaps, but no devils.' The historian says that these are facts because that is the way in which he has been taught to think. But the devil-fearer says that the presence of devils is a fact, because that is the way in which he has been taught to think. The historian thinks it a wrong way; but wrong ways of thinking are just as much historical facts as right ones, and, no less than they, determine the situation (always a thought situation) in which the man who shares them is placed. The hardness of the fact consists in the man's inability to think of his situation otherwise. The compulsion which the devil-haunted mountains exercise on the man who would not cross them consists in the fact that he cannot help believing in the devils. Sheer superstition, no doubt: but this superstition is a fact, and the crucial fact in the situation we are considering (IH, 317).

For an account of Hume's philosophy of history see D. F. Norton, 'History and Philosophy in Hume's Thought' in D. F. Norton and R. H. Popkin, eds., *David Hume: Philosophical Historian* (New York, Bobbs-Merril, 1965); for an account of Collingwood's critique of Bradley see Lionell Rubinoff, 'The Autonomy of History: Collingwood's Critique of F. H. Bradley's Copernican Revolution in Historical Knowledge', in *Philosophy After F. H. Bradley*, edited by James Bradley (Bristol, Thoemmes Press, 1996).

19 To some extent the rejection of any notion of nomologicality in history may be due to an over-reaction to Hempel's claim for methodological unity.

20 A further reason for the relative neglect of this third conception of history may be due

to the fact that it is often associated with Collingwood's later thought and in particular with an historicist or relativist turn in which Collingwood obliterates the boundaries between philosophy and history. Toulmin, for instance, argues that in this later period of thought Collingwood rejected epistemological pluralism in favour of historical relativism as he replaced the claim for the relativity of epistemological standpoints to disciplines, with a claim for the relativity of epistemological standpoints to historical periods (S. Toulmin, 'Conceptual Change and the Problem of Relativity', in *Critical Essays in the Philosophy of R. G. Collingwood*, Oxford, Clarendon Press, 1972). It is partly to avoid an unwanted identification of the role of philosophy and metaphysics that an attempt has been made to make clear demarcations between the subject matter of history and that of philosophy by denying that historical explanations apply to intersubjectively shared norms which provide the background for the actions of individuals as opposed to those specific and more detailed considerations which stand in the foreground of action. Whereas I would agree with those who sustain that metaphysics is best defined as the study of the absolute presuppositions which structure and make possible disciplines, rather than as the study of historical epochs (see A. Oldfield's 'Metaphysics and History in Collingwood's Thought' and Rex Martin's 'Collingwood's Claim that Metaphysics is an Historical Discipline' both in *Philosophy, History and Civilization*, Boucher, Connelly and Modood. I would also want to argue that there is a great deal of scope for substantive history in Collingwood. In fact, Collingwood often seems to treat intersubjectively shared beliefs as suppressed premises in the practical argument that the historian reconstructs in the attempt to understand the actions of historical agents. To return to the example of the devil fearer one might say that the agent who refuses to cross the mountain chain might express his reluctance to do so by saying that he will not go because there are devils in the mountains: such an agent is unlikely to voice his reluctance by saying that he is the kind of human being who believes that devils are part of the world's ontology and since there happens to be devils in this particular mountain, he will not attempt the crossing. It is the suppressed epistemological premise that devils are part of the furniture of the world that the historian must make explicit if he is to understand historically.

21   It is important to point out that although Collingwood espoused the thesis of the logical priority of the idea of history over the idea of nature (according to which representations of nature are part of the conceptual articulation of reality in any given historical period) he did not believe that the relativity of concepts and attitudes to historical contexts, entailed another and quite different thesis, i.e., historical relativism (the claim that no rational comparison across historical periods is possible or rational). Collingwood often made comparison across historical periods. In *The Idea of History*, for instance, he traces the development of the concept of history from the Greek period to his own days and he leaves the reader in no doubt about which, amongst the conceptions of history which happened to be prevalent in different times, is superior. He never claims, for instance, that scientific history is 'our' way of thinking about history, the way in which we do things here and now, but rather that the description of history which is found in scientific history is the right way of thinking about history, period. In other words, Collingwood does not, as he is sometimes accused of doing, believe that historical relativity (the thesis concerning the relativity of knowledge claims to history) entails historical relativism (the thesis concerning the non comparability of knowledge claims), a criticism voiced quite powerfully by Toulmin (S. Toulmin, 'Conceptual Change and the Problem of Relativity', *Critical Essays in the Philosophy of R. G. Collingwood*, edited by M. Krausz, Oxford, Clarendon Press, 1972, p. 213). Having provided a historical survey of conceptions of history he proceeds to

compare what he refers to as 'common sense', scissors-and-paste' and 'scientific' history on the basis of their ability to do justice to the goal of understanding the past: the different conceptions of this discipline, therefore, are assessed on the basis of their ability to deliver historical understanding and inadequate conceptions of history are discarded by following a procedure which is dialectical in nature.

22 P. Gardiner, 'The Objects of Historical Knowledge', *Philosophy* 27 (1952).

23 For an account of the criteria of the identity of thought see H. Saari, 'R. G. Collingwood on the Identity of Thought', *Dialogue: Canadian Philosophical Review* 28 (1989), and my 'Collingwood on Re-enactment and the Identity of Thought' in *Journal of the History of Philosophy*, XXXVIII (2000). For an account which emphasises the Fregean flavour of Collingwood's account of re-enactment see van der Dussen's 'The Philosophical Context of Collingwood's Re-enactment Theory', *International Studies in Philosophy* XXVII:2, (1995).

24 For a rejection of the charge of methodological individualism see W. H. Dray's 'Collingwood's Historical Individualism' in *Canadian Journal of Philosophy* 10, 1980 and his *History as Re-enactment: R. G. Collingwood's Idea of History* (Oxford, Clarendon Press, 1995), 184 ff.

25 The discovery of *The Principles of History* has enabled one to know that the discussion of historical inference, and the illustration of how it works in the case of John Doe, did not belong to the original text of *The Idea of History*. The discussion of historical inference, which appears in *The Idea of History*, part V, §3, was the first chapter of *The Principles of History*. It was Knox's editorial decision to insert it in part V of IH. On this point see D. Boucher's '*The Principles of History* and the Cosmology Conclusion to *The Idea of Nature*' in *Collingwood Studies* 2 (1995), especially, 171.

COLLINGWOOD
CORNER

Collingwood and his Contemporaries: Responses to Critics 1918-1928

JAMES CONNELLY
Southampton Institute

This collection of reviews represents Collingwood's response to some of his contemporaries over the period 1918-1928, the time in which, having rejected the realism of his early career, he gradually worked out, through intensive study of the Italian idealists such as Croce, Gentile and de Ruggiero, a philosophy of his own. In so doing he was indebted to these thinkers, but critically re-thought their work in constructing his own philosophical views.

Collingwood does not hesitate in being sharply critical of those who in his view committed fundamental errors in interpretation or philosophical argument; equally he can be generous, as he is towards May Sinclair and R. F. A. Hoernlé. But, over and above particular comments and criticisms, in reading these reviews, it is fascinating that a common theme emerges from these reviews, a theme which relates directly to the question what philosophy is, and what its proper mode of expression should be, the topics which he later systematised in *An Essay on Philosophical Method*. There he writes that philosophers' "only excuse for writing is that they mean to make a clean breast, first to themselves, and then to their readers, if they have any", because "Every piece of philosophical writing is primarily addressed by the author to himself . . . the philosopher . . . must always be confessing his difficulties, whereas the historian is always to some extent concealing them" (*EPM*, 209-11). Collingwood's point is partly that any worthwhile philosophy must express a definite point of view – something he finds lacking in both Windelband and Gunn – and also that a philosophical point of view cannot be acquired second hand simply by reading books. To learn from other philosophers' books "it is not enough that we should in a general way be thoughtful or intelligent; not enough even that we should be interested and skilled in philosophy. We must be equipped, not for any and every philosophical enterprise, but for the one which we are undertaking. What we get by reading any book is conditioned by what we bring to it; and in philosophy no one can get much good by reading the works of a writer whose problems have not already arisen spontaneously in the reader's mind" (*EPM*, 216). Thus, in his review of Santayana, he comments that "you cannot acquire a point of view by reading books"; and this is the burden of his rather polite criticism of Sinclair, where he remarks that she has written "a book about books – a very good one – rather than a new work . . . She has mastered the literature of the subject: may we hope that she will write her next philosophical work in some place where the literature is inaccessible, and write it about the subject itself?"

Collingwood's review of Santayana's *Realm of Essence* brings out another aspect of his views concerning the nature and proper mode of expression of philosophy. Santayana's point of view is "held like a great glittering jewel in the writer's hand and scrutinized under every kind of light, turned this way and that and studied in all its aspects as Monet studied his haystack under every hour's varying illumination." Collingwood understands why this manner of writing was adopted, perhaps as a response to the dialectical treatment of the philosophical subject matter in Hegel and those following that manner (including Collingwood himself in *Speculum Mentis*). But this alternative manner of philosophical writing has defects which extend beyond mere matters of style:

> The real fault, I think, lies in his conception of what a philosophy should be. For him, it is a jewel: a thing to be polished and rounded and perfected and then offered to the world as one of a potentially infinite number of systems, all valid and all legitimate, because each has achieved a genuine intuition of an essence. That is a good description of a poem; it is a bad description of a philosophy.

This was the theme Collingwood addressed in strikingly similar terms in the final chapter of *An Essay on Philosophical Method*. This chapter was entitled "philosophy as a branch of literature" and he writes there that:

> the principles on which the philosopher uses language are those of poetry; but what he writes is not poetry but prose. From the point of view of literary form, this means that whereas the poet yields himself to every suggestion that his language makes, and so produces word-patterns whose beauty is a sufficient reason for their existence, the philosopher's word-patterns are constructed only to reveal the thought which they express, and are valuable not in themselves but as means to that end. The prose-writer's art is an art that must conceal itself, and produce not a jewel that is looked at for its own beauty but a crystal in whose depths the thought can be seen without distortion or confusion; and the philosophical writer in especial follows the trade not of a jeweller but of a lens-grinder. (*EPM*, 214)

Whether or not these words were written as a particular response to Santayana or as a consequence of a general meditation on philosophical style I cannot say; but at the very least Santayana's writing provides us with a clear example of the sort of target at which Collingwood was aiming.

Reverting to Collingwood's relations with the older British idealists and with the Italian idealists, it is instructive to contrast the reviews of Wildon Carr and Bosanquet. In the former, Collingwood is sympathetic to the enterprise and generous in reconstructing Carr's argument; in the latter, by contrast, Bosanquet is roundly castigated for a failure to understand the authors he presumes to criticise. The tone and content is not dissimilar to his responses to the critics of the "new idealism" in his contribution to 1923 Aristotelian Society symposium "Can the New Idealism dispense with Mysticism" in which Collingwood firmly corrects the misunderstandings he finds in Evelyn Underhill's account and simultaneously presents a lucid and positive re-statement of the leading doctrines of Croce, Gentile and de Ruggiero.

Collingwood's relationship with Bernard Bosanquet is an interesting one. Bosanquet taught his father at University College. But the younger Collingwood often tended, where he took notice of Bosanquet, to be sharply critical. For example, he frequently refers to Bosanquet's quip about history being nothing more than "the doubtful story of successive events"; in general, he appears to regard Bradley as a superior source of philosophical insight, writing on his philosophy of history, logic and metaphysics. If we return to Bosanquet's commentary on "the extremes in contemporary philosophy" it is instructive to note two things. The first is that although Collingwood had repudiated realism by this date, at least in the sense that he no longer regarded himself as a disciple of Cook Wilson, he nonetheless took a considerable interest in the work of Alexander and Whitehead, and corresponded with Alexander from the mid-1920s until his death in 1938. In 1935 Alexander provided a testimonial for Collingwood's successful application for the Waynflete chair of Metaphysical Philosophy. The second is that, especially in the early 1920s, Collingwood was doing a tremendous amount of work on the Italian idealists. During this period he produced a translation of de Ruggiero's 'Scienza come esperienza assoluta', wrote 'Croce's Philosophy of History'; composed *Libellus de Generatione*, translated de Ruggiero's *Modern Philosophy* and gave lectures on de Ruggiero's philosophy. He revised and translated Croce's *Aesthetic* and contemplated publishing a translation of de Ruggiero's *Filosofia del Cristianesimo*. In 1923 he delivered 'Can the New Idealism Dispense with Mysticism?' In 1925 he was translating Croce's *Autobiography* and in 1926 de Ruggiero's *History of European Liberalism*. His critical response to realism and his preoccupation with the agenda of Italian philosophy were two sides of the same coin; Bosanquet's book marked what for Collingwood was an ill-informed intrusion onto the territory that Collingwood had made his own and he responded vigorously to the territorial challenge.

Collingwood clearly had no time for Russell's ethics or for his logic (*An Autobiography*, 35-6); and his realist epistemology struck him as incoherent. Nonetheless it appears that Collingwood considered Russell's work as not entirely devoid of merit. In *An Autobiography* he is described as "a gifted and accomplished writer"; and elsewhere he receives praise which can only be described as fulsome. For example, in his review of *Mysticism and Logic*, Collingwood states that "such essays as that on the notion of cause ought to be read by every one who has any interest in philosophy"; this judgement was re-affirmed twenty years later in "On the So-called Idea of Causation" where Collingwood refers to Russell, "whose brilliant paper 'on the notion of cause' . . . is worth everything else put together that has been written on the subject during the present century" (*A,* 108); this discussion, together with the affirmation of Collingwood's debt to Russell, later formed Part IIIc of *An Essay on Metaphysics.*

These reviews have the considerable merit of providing a window on the development of Collingwood's thought; on careful examination they illustrate well different facets of his approach to philosophical method and substantive philosophy and metaphysics.

Review of May Sinclair, *A Defence of Idealism: Some Questions and Conclusions,* Macmillan, 1917. *Oxford Magazine,* 15/2/18, p. 173.

The greatest novelist of the last generation was the brother of one of its most eminent philosophers. Miss Sinclair doubles the parts: a novelist of repute and ability, she has come forward as a philosopher too. Not that there is anything new in that. We have long suffered from a plague of novelist-theologians and philosopher-playwrights. But Miss Sinclair "keeps things separate;" her novels are novels, not tracts; and when she sits down to philosophize, she asks for nothing but a clear fire and the rigour of the game.

We said advisedly that she doubles the parts: for if her novels betray the extent of her admiration for the one brother, her *Defence of Idealism* shows on almost every page the influence of the other. She is no follower of William James, but her racy style and vivid expression have evidently been learnt in great measure from him; none the less that they are weapons which she mercilessly employs against himself. Even in method she has one striking affinity with James. It was always his object to analyse the temper of philosophers: to lay, if anything, more emphasis on their feelings than on their assertions. Miss Sinclair is very sensitive to this element in philosophy; a melodramatic gesture always catches her eye and leads her to look for a flaw in the thought which it expresses. On the other hand, just because she uses this method well, she is never so down on James as when he abuses it. Her comment on a classical passage deserves itself to become a classic. "Think of the sheer terrorism of the performance. Could you wonder if, covered with that six-shooter, Professor James's audience plumped for Pragmatism before it had heard a single argument? Each member of it must have registered an inward vow: 'Tough-minded? *I'll* be *that!*' "

With regard to Miss Sinclair's own philosophical temper, it might be said that a book which proclaims itself a defence of anything ending in -ism was lacking on just that point. But this would be a little unfair. The spiritual monism which Miss Sinclair calls idealism is no one-sided doctrine. It is willing to accept all the assertions of pluralism, while protesting against its denials. Indeed, there are moments when "our monist" shows himself so broad-minded in his assent that we begin to wonder what he will do with it all. And certainly the final synthesis is inconclusive. Of this the author makes no secret. She criticizes much – and her criticism is always thoughtful and never unjust – but her positive construction amounts to little more than suggestions for future development.

Finally, since Miss Sinclair asks for the rigour of the game, it must be said that the book is a trifle chaotic. The thread on which the various criticisms are strung is slender; the author so enjoys herself over Bergson, or the pragmatists, or the New Realism, that we often lose sight of any connected argument. It is a book about books – a very good one – rather than a new work. We should not complain of this were it not that Miss Sinclair has the root of the matter in her and is capable of doing new work. She has mastered the literature of the subject: may we hope that she will write her next philosophical work in some place where the literature is inaccessible, and write it about the subject itself?

Review of Bertrand Russell, *Mysticism and Logic*, Allen & Unwin, 1918. *Oxford Magazine*, 14/2/19, p. 129.

These essays, written at various dates from 1902 to 1914, illustrate not only many different sides of Mr Russell's philosophy, but also more than one stage in its development. The earlier essays – the rhetorical "Free Man's Worship" and "The Study of Mathematics", with its emphasis on the superiority, from an intellectual point of view, of the mathematician's ideal world to the confused and confusing "second best" world of "real life" – are chiefly interesting as a foil to the later, as showing how much the writer has gained, since they were written, in outlook and style. The later and more important essays are too varied to be adequately described in a short review; and it seems best to select one or two points for a closer consideration.

Mr Russell insists, in more than one essay, that philosophy must abandon the "unprogressive methods" which it has hitherto employed; and maintains that this reform of method is to be effected by the banishment from philosophy of ethics. This demand may have two meanings; it may mean that conduct is not a fit subject for philosophy – that ethics is a pseudo-philosophy: or that "ethical considerations" ought to have no place in metaphysics; that philosophers ought not to consider questions of fact by appealing to deliverances of the moral consciousness. Mr Russell's meaning is, of course, the latter. He holds that philosophers have "hitherto" tended to describe things not as they are, but as we think they ought to be – or even simply as we should like them to be. This would be an excellent text for a study in the history of philosophy; but Mr Russell does not so treat it. He tells us in one place that the philosophers who assert mind to be the basis of the universe do so because such an assertion gives them "the cosy feeling that every place is like home;" and it is only from such casual accusations that we learn what exactly he means by the ill effects of ethics upon philosophy.

Now Mr Russell is right in saying that a cosy feeling is not the true end of philosophy. But is he right in identifying "ethical considerations" with the desire for a cosy feeling? He is quite serious in this identification. "Ethics" (meaning morality) "is in origin the art of recommending to others the sacrifices required for cooperation with oneself." (p. 108); and he develops this view in several passages. Apparently Mr Russell's moral philosophy, unlike his theory of knowledge, belongs to the crudest type of evolutionary empiricist theories; and consequently his attack on ethical metaphysics stands or falls with theories of that type.

A minor point is worth mentioning in this connexion. In contrasting the educational value of science with that of literature and art generally, Mr Russell says that in art "the men of Greece and the renaissance did better than any men do now. The triumphs of former ages . . . actually increase the difficulty of fresh triumphs by rendering originality harder of attainment: not only is artistic achievement not cumulative, but it even seems to depend on a certain freshness and *naïveté* of impulse and vision which civilization tends to destroy." This assertion seems of a piece with Mr Russell's belief in the unprogressive nature of all previous philosophy.

These faults do not outweigh the great value and charm of the book as a whole. No one can make mathematical problems more attractive to the layman than Mr Russell; and such essays as that on the notion of cause ought to be read by every one who has any interest in philosophy.

Review of Wilhelm Windelband, *An Introduction to Philosophy*, Fisher Unwin, 1921. *Oxford Magazine*, 8/12/21, p. 158.

Detailed study of the history of thought sometimes appears almost to extinguish, instead of feeding, the flame of thought itself. Fear of committing himself to a philosophical position (candidly expressed in the preface, which tells us that "the book is in no sense an introduction to a special philosophical system") prevents the author from ever talking a definite line, and almost every statement is "hedged". The result is a book full of learning, but composed of an alternation between disjointed historical facts and vacillating reflections upon them. And ultimately a system is maintained, but an eclectic and confused one. There is no such thing as philosophy in general that is not this or that philosophy; and an introduction to philosophy is only worth writing when an author who thinks his views are worth stating states them clearly and simply. On the other hand the aim of collecting "a general view of philosophical problems and the tendencies of the various attempts to solve them" might have been achieved by writing a beginner's history of philosophy; and it is much to be deplored that instead of doing this, which he could have done well, so eminent a man as Windelband has devoted himself to an enterprise foredoomed to failure.

Review of Bernard Bosanquet, *The Meeting of Extremes in Contemporary Philosophy*. Macmillan, 1921. *Oxford Magazine*, 2/3/22, p. 271.

A new book of Dr Bosanquet is an event; and happily not so rare an event as it was. He now gives us a criticism of a certain attitude which he finds exemplified in both the extremes of philosophy today, "neo-realism" and "neo-idealism;" an ethical, humanistic, empiricist or positivist attitude which he contrasts with his own absolutism, the "speculative philosophy which penetrates and apprehends the unity which is grasped by faith" and asserts the infinite or absolute "beyond" the process of our thinking. His treatment of the neo-realists, especially Prof. Alexander, is sympathetic, painstaking and just: that of the neo-idealists is less satisfying. Only two are recognised, Croce and Gentile: and it is surprisingly assumed that their views are identical. Nor do our surprises end here. Neo-idealism, we are told, is simply another radical empiricism; it preaches the novelty of thought without its necessity, the Spencerian evanescence of evil, and the negation of transcendence, not merely in the sense of the unknowable thing-in-itself transcending thought, but in the very different sense of the object of thought that transcends immediacy or intuition. This, to quote a phrase of Dr Bosanquet's own, is "amazing, incredible, if it were not there in black and white." We are driven to believe that he wholly misunderstood Croce and Gentile when they deny "all" transcendence (all possible forms of the unknowable), and overlooked their central doctrines of the *a priori* synthesis and the concept as an "*un di là*" of intuition. If he has, we can understand his evident impatience with them; but we cannot accept his picture of their philosophy as even remotely like the original.

Review of J. A. Gunn, *Modern French Philosophy*, Fisher Unwin, 1922. *Oxford Magazine*, 7/12/22, p. 146.

Dr. Gunn has given us a thorough and painstaking study of French Philosophy since Comte. It is a singularly interesting period, and one which ought to be more familiar to students of philosophy than it is; they are apt to select a single figure from it and treat this, in defiance of facts, as an isolated phenomenon. Now that Dr. Gunn has published this work, there will be no excuse for failing to see the period in proper historical perspective. The book is workmanlike and adequate; but it has defects. The arrangements breaks up what is really a single narrative into a number of parallel narratives in which there is necessarily a great deal of repetition and loss of clearness; it is an interesting experiment, but it is certainly not successful. And Dr. Gunn's habit is perhaps too much to lay equal stress on everything, rather than to select for emphasis what is most important. Hence the book reads dully, and often fails to do justice to the real merit of the writers described. But in spite of these defects the book will prove extremely useful to students of philosophy.

Review of R. F. A. Hoernlé, *Matter, Life, Mind and God*, Methuen 1923. *Oxford Magazine*, 7/6/23.

Few of our leading philosophers understand how to write a book. As a rule, when they publish, they either reprint a scratch collection of technical essays on points of detail, or else expand one such essay into a volume. In either case they write as specialists for specialists, and seem hardly to suspect that a printed book addressed only to specialists is thrown away. Professor Hoernlé knows better, and the present work is a model of what one kind of philosophical book should be. It consists of a course of lecturers given in Newcastle not to University students but to an audience united only by a desire "to understand whither the reflections of leading thinkers of the day are tending on such persistent problems as Matter and Life, Mind and God." Hence the book is untechnical in expression, and in exposition aims at including only what is of prime importance. The result is that it admirably succeeds in its purpose, and we know nothing better as a guide to the subjects with which it deals.

The main body of the book consists of exposition of others' views, the author claiming only the part of an "intelligent showman". He makes an admirable showman, sympathetic and penetrating, always attentive to the best in the creatures lodged in his cages, and endowed with the born showman's knack of forgetting himself in the interest of his show. But there is more in the book than a mere philosophical circus; the exposition is strung together on a philosophical thread which runs through the whole work. The author's watchword is the Platonic adjective "synoptic"; and the method followed is the synthesis of activities – physical science, biological science, psychological science, religion – each of which is by itself presumed to attain one fragment of the truth, to contribute one element to the whole and complete view of things. This is the ideal of the book; and the exposition is inspired by the hope of discovering in these various fields of thought a tendency to convergence, a tendency in each separate field to overcome, by its own internal dialectic, its one sidedness and thus its implicit contradiction of the others. Thus, Professor Hoernlé finds in Dr. Whitehead's attack on "matter" a spontaneous movement on the part of physical science towards the position of idealistic philosophy; much as Professor Wildon Carr finds grist for the idealist's mill in Einstein's attack on absolute space and time. We should like to agree, but we cannot. All the vices of materialism are, we fear, compatible with a position like that of Dr. Whitehead (not that we accuse Dr. Whitehead himself of indulging in them); and the realists do not seem convinced by Professor Wildon Carr's thesis. Is not the idea that the different departments of thought, if left to themselves, will converge to a common result, a mere baseless assumption, a relic of the Spencerian "evanescence of evil?" Is it not at least as likely that their divergences will be, to use M. Bergson's word, exasperated? And though synopsis is doubtless the philosopher's duty, though he is bound to do justice to every form of thought, may there not be forms of thought for which a synoptic philosophy "finds room" only in the sense in which a well-governed country finds room for criminals – in a prison cell? For all our enjoyment of Professor Hoernlé's learned, readable and charming pages, these doubts continue to afflict us.

Review of J. B. S. Haldane *Daedalus, or Science and the Future* and Bertrand Russell, *Icarus, or the Future of Science*. Kegan Paul, 1924. *Oxford Magazine*, 15/05/24, p. 456.

Vaticination is an art, not a science; and prophets predict one thing rather than another not because there is adequate ground for the choice, but because it takes them that way. When scientists prophesy, they think that they are relying on their scientific equipment, but in fact they are simply giving free rein to their temperament. It is natural, therefore, that Mr Haldane's predictions should be sanguine and Mr Russell's melancholic. Mr Haldane, following the early Wellsian method of assuming that the tendencies of the immediate past will continue to develop along the tangent, presents us with a future in which the industrial, urban and scientific elements of modern life are intensified to the progressive exclusion of their opposites. Mr Russell, agreeing that this would be delightful if it could happen, retorts that it cannot happen because man has always a bad angel, the State, frustrating the efforts of his good angel, the Scientist, and turning them to its own nefarious ends; and, therefore, the future will develop by a centripetal collapse along the radius. To criticise would be to break butterflies on the wheel. The courteous reader will thank both writers for their pleasant and stimulating essays, and say nothing about the *naiveté* with which Mr Haldane assumes the supremacy of science over all other forms of experience, or the now familiar crudity of Mr Russell's ethical and political theories.

Review of H. Wildon Carr, *A Theory of Monads*, Macmillan, 1922. *Hibbert Journal*, vol 23, no 2, 1925, pp. 380-382.

Professor Wildon Carr points out in his preface that this book is not, as it title might seem to imply, a systematic work, but rather a collection of essays which group themselves round a central point of view. But it would be a mistake to read them as independent essays, for many of them contain brief and, taken in isolation, cryptic references to subjects fully dealt with in later passages; so that the book must read as a whole in order to do justice to the author's point of view. That point of view may be roughly indicated by saying that it is a new monadology; but one whose motive is not to revive the doctrine of Leibniz, but rather to weld into a single whole the results of four conceptions, each of which has deeply impressed the author's mind: Bergson's conception of creative evolution, Croce's conception of imaginative intuition as an autonomous activity logically prior to thought, Gentile's conception of the Spirit as pure act, and the theory of relativity. The ultimate reality, as Professor Carr conceived it, is life; and life means activity, a process of self-making. This process generates a distinction between activity in itself, in its immediacy, and the duration of activity, its self-identity through change, and in this distinction Professor Carr finds the source of the distinction between body and mind, the body being that which changes, the perishable, the activity which expends itself in acting, and the mind that which endures, the activity which realises itself in acting. Body and mind are thus not two things connected by parallelism or interactionism, but the inseparable terms of a dialectical antithesis which arises out of the nature of life. The chapter which expounds this conception is possibly the most original, and certainly to the present reviewer the most stimulating, in the book. Life, so conceived, is not an attribute but the substance of each individual monad; and each monad exists in itself and for the others, that is to say, it enjoys (as Professor Alexander would say) its own body-mind activity, and in this activity mirrors the whole universe. Each monad, in other words, makes the other monads the objects of its knowledge; but it is not an object to itself, it does not apprehend itself as a monad, for what it apprehends is the unique perspective of the universe as seen from its own point of view. This seeing of the universe is deduced from the conception of life itself, under the Bergsonian name of "attention to life"; the monad's consciousness so far as its life evolves a consciousness, is an attention to "the action which is forming before it," a self-preparation "to receive the external influences reaction to which is the primal necessity of life." This consciousness is essentially memory, which is not the "present recollection of a non-existent past," but the actual existence of the past in the present, as constituting present experience. But memory is essentially imagination; what is present to a remembering mind is altogether imagery; and imagery is the fundamental form of intellectual life, being itself based upon and expressive of a pre-intellectual life of emotion. Reality is thus life, and all knowledge is, therefore the knowledge by life of life, – that is to say, not of things but of processes, activities, events. Knowledge is always historical knowledge; and what appears to physical analysis as a material universe is actually experienced as, and actually is, a system of event co-ordinated in a frame of reference which is the monad's perspective of the world.

This account of Professor Carr's thesis is arrived at by putting together what seem to be the crucial points from scattered passages up and down the book; and if it fails to do him justice, we must plead in extenuation that he has left us to do the work of systematising for ourselves, preferring to put into our hands a mass of detail – always interesting detail, and handled in an interesting way – in which the principles of his philosophy are illustrated. There is so much in his position with which we agree, that it is perhaps best to deal at once with the point in regard to which we find most difficulty; and this is the conception of the monad. The monad does not apprehend itself as a monad (p. 53); it is both in-itself and for-another (p. 57), but not, we are left to infer, for itself. Now if this be so – and unless it be so the conception of the monad is meaningless – what is the good of saying that we must "direct our study on the self" (p. 90)? The monad appears to be an eye which is invisible to itself; it sees its world, but in the nature of the case it cannot see itself, and we need not trouble to recommend it to try. Now, surely this destroys the very possibility of a theory of monads. The whole of that theory consists in the discovery that I am a monad; but if I am a monad, how can I know that I am a monad? Only by getting outside my own monadic point of view and seeing it as one among similar points of view. No monad can be a monadologist; one cannot be a monadologist until one has transcended the status of a monad. No doubt this is only a restatement of the old difficulty about inter-monadic communication, which the author deals with by pointing out that nothing can be common to two minds unless it exists in terms of each mind taken separately (p. 35), so that one person only understands another so far as his individual intelligence enables him to do so: thus although monads have no windows, each is to the other, when intelligently regarded, an intelligible spirit. Still, however, could a mind which was not an intelligible object to itself understand another mind? And if not, must we not infer that not only the possession of a monadological philosophy but the possession of any knowledge whatever depends upon the monad's becoming "for-itself."

The difficulty reappears in the conception of "attention to life." This cannot mean "attention to the agent's own activity," for that would make the monad an object to itself; nor "attention to the objective circumstances in which the agent finds himself," for that is expressly repudiated (pp. 150-151); nor yet "attention to the agent's emotions and reflexes," for these never become "chosen and free" (p. 150), however much one attends to them. And it reappears once more in the view that matter is a "diminution of life." Why should life suffer this diminution? Because of the narrowing of the intellectual outlook to the immediate problem of action; but this implies either that the outlook is an outlook upon objective circumstances, in which case the argument is circular, or that it is the agent's self-consciousness, in which case again the monad is "for-itself."

Perhaps the fundamental question is the meaning of activity. Professor Carr comments on the electrical theory of matter by saying that "in physics, as in metaphysics, the ultimate concept of reality is activity" (p. 291). But, after all, the electrical theory of matter is a theory of *matter*, and matter is by definition the opposite of activity: and to make matter itself into an activity is merely to conjure up the night in which all cows are black. If, as Professor Carr would clearly permit us to do, we may put our difficulty into Hegelian terminology, we would express a doubt as to whether the function of negativity is sufficiently emphasised in his dialectic. Just as monadism must be negated in order to reach monadology, so the physical account of matter and the biological analysis of life must be, always in the Hegelian sense, negated in order to reach the philosophical concept of the pure act.

But we do not mean to suggest that Professor Carr could not have removed these difficulties if he had chosen to present his thesis in a more systematic form; and it would certainly be hypercritical to insist on them without expressing our high appreciation of the value and interest of the book as a whole.

Review of George Santayana, *The Realm of Essence*. Constable, 1928. *New Adelphi*, Vol. 1, 1927-8, pp. 357-60.

Any philosophy is a point of view taken up by the philosopher towards things in general; and the complete statement of a particular philosophy consists partly of sailing directions to persons desirous of arriving at this particular point of view, partly of descriptions explaining what things look like to one who has reached it. For the beginner, the main thing is the sailing-directions: and here a great advantage lies with the ancient Greek, the mediaeval European, and the Oriental of every period, who learn their philosophy in a school of regular and even ascetic discipline. You cannot acquire a point of view by reading books. You must be schooled to it: long personal contact with people possessing it, and subjection of the will and affections to its indispensable and affections to its cultivation, are its indispensable approaches. European thought, since the break-up of the mediaeval tradition, has lost this advantage, and has almost ceased to realise its loss, complacently cherishing the illusion that philosophy (or, for that matter, anything) can be learnt solely from books.

But with the loss of this traditional discipline has arisen a new technique in the writing of philosophical books, a technique, one might fancy, deliberately intended to compensate for it. Whereas earlier works were all esoteric, in the sense that they required a trained reader, and became intelligible only when the point of view which they represented had already been reached, these new works contained in themselves the sailing-directions necessary to bring the reader to the point of view of the writer's philosophy. Thus the point of view keeps shifting throughout the book: the writer leads the reader by the hand from one view point to another until the mountain of his thought has been scaled and they stand together on the summit.

This method of writing philosophy reached its culmination in the hands of Hegel; and since his time there has been a reaction. People came to realise that the method involved an over-estimation of the power of books. If you cannot acquire a point of view by reading books, but only by long practical discipline, you cannot, as the Hegelian dialectic bids you do, acquire scores of them, one to every few pages, as you sit in an armchair. So, by substituting literature for life, the dialectical movement of thought becomes what Bradley called "an unearthly ballet of bloodless categories". The reaction against Hegel's method is seen in its purest and most extreme form in a book like this of Mr Santayana. It is as long as Hegel's original encyclopaedia, but it consists of a single point of view, described and re-described and described again, never altered or approached or receded from, but held like a great glittering jewel in the writer's hand and scrutinized under every kind of light, turned this way and that and studied in all its aspects as Monet studied his haystack under every hour's varying illumination.

Impressionism is apt to breed impatience in a spectator. Critics might have urged Monet to leave his haystack alone and get on to something else. Yet impressionism justified itself; that way of studying haystacks did prove useful. And Mr Santayana's philosophical impressionism has this in its favour: that, even if a reader feels that all this could have been said in a few pages, the very elaboration of the thing makes it impossible, or nearly impossible, for any reader to fail of arriving at the author's point of view. If you must rely on books, if you must make philosophy literary, you must take the consequences: that is to say, you must write in the best possible prose the most elaborate exposition of the very simplest ideas, and feel your labour well spent if, at the end of one volume, you have stated one idea.

The idea of essence is a very simple idea, and Mr Santayana has thought it out with the utmost lucidity, and expounded it with that elegance and clarity which are the admiration, envy and despair of other philosophical writers. Plato has accustomed us to think of essences, and to recognise in triangularity or justice a "form" (an essence, Mr Santayana would say) exemplified in triangular things or just actions, but having its own eternal being independently of anything or action whatever, "itself by itself." Mr Santayana would say that Plato was so far right, but would add that there is an essence, just as eternal, of blueness or dog-in-the-manger-ish-ness and even that there is an essence of the particular sound-group which I heard just now – the peculiar rhythm of raindrops on the window combined with the peculiar rise and fall of the wind's howl in the chimney – which was embodied in an actually existing thing, this morning's storm, exactly as justice may be embodied in an actual legal decision, and, before and after being so embodied, has, exactly as much as that, its own proper eternal disembodied existence. Thus the question which Plato raises in the *Parmenides*, "*Of what* are there essences?" Mr Santayana answers, boldly and without hesitation, "of everything concerning which the question could possibly be asked". Is there an essence of mud? The fact that you can ask the question proves that there is. Is there an essence of evil, of injustice, of out-of-tuneness? Yes, for the same reason. Whenever we ask "What is this thing?" and answer "blue," or "a gold watch," or "an error," or "Septuagesima," our answer is the name of an essence. Essences are "whats," if we may appeal to the traditional distinction between the *that* and the *what* – the fact *that* a thing exists and the question *what* it is.

So far, no reader has any option but to follow Mr Santayana, with gratitude for his firm grasp and lucid statement of an important, if elementary, idea. In philosophy the most important ideas are generally the most elementary. But it is part of the author's method that he does not envisage or anticipate or meet any criticisms whatever. His procedure is to state his doctrine, dogmatically, in its rounded perfection, for the reader to take or leave. Because the reader accepts it (how can he help himself? – it is so reasonable, and so well expressed) the reader will accept its consequences, and will adjust his other ideas to it, not it to his other ideas. Thus, to take one example of such adjustment, it can be easily shown that essence have no implications. Therefore, the three-corneredness of a triangle (which, of course, is an essence embodied in the triangle) is not implied by the other essence, its three-sidedness: three-corneredness and three-sidedness are just two different essences which I happen to have observed in the same thing – the triangle. Here, perhaps, the reader will begin to bluster: "Come, come: you are denying the *a priori* element in knowledge, and asking me to join you in reducing *a priori* certainties to *a posteriori* observations." Oh no, Mr Santayana replies, I admit the reality of the *a priori*; but every instinct and organ has its history, just as ever custom has, and once the organ is formed, it imposes *a priori* certain response on the body and certain ideas on the mind. The *a priori*, then is only psychologically necessary, and this necessity is a mere biological fact. This doctrine, which poses as an explanation of the *a priori*, is really its negation. Mr Santayana has made mathematics impossible.

Then what about natural science? He has made that impossible, too. The processes of nature are "a perpetual genesis of the unwarrantable out of the contingent," and though this process may contain repetitions, these repetitions are never necessary in themselves, nor known by us as necessary; we merely learn to expect them. That is to say, a crudely empiricist denial of logical necessity leads to a crudely empiricist denial of natural necessity. Natural change is simply the disembodiment of one essence and the embodiment of another: as no essence has implications, there is no reason in the essences themselves why any transition should take place rather than any other, or, indeed, than none at all.

After this, it is not surprising that philosophy becomes equally impossible. Logic and ethics evidently become part of biology (which is a natural science), and metaphysics seems either to disappear altogether, being in one place frankly called a fiction, or, being elsewhere identified with the study of essence, to become another name for science. Kant's three questions, How is pure mathematics possible? How is the pure science of nature possible? How is pure metaphysics possible? are all three answered in the same way – it is *not* possible. Caligula's wish that all mankind had a single head, to be chopped off with one blow, here comes true of all kinds of knowledge.

This, it might be replied, is an over-statement. Knowledge is not exterminated: it is reduced to the observation of things and the intuition of their essences. That is to say, we are assisting at a restatement of ordinary empiricism. But observation of things and intuition of their essences is not knowledge: it is only that *part* of knowledge which is not thinking; and that part by itself is not knowledge. But Mr Santayana might here accuse me of the grossest stupidity: do I not see that what I call thinking he calls intuiting essences? I do: and I see also that to call it that is to call it by a name which deprives it of its very essence. For thought, too, has an essence: and its essence lies in regarding its objects not as isolated entities, but as mutually related within a whole which implies them as they imply each other. No, Mr Santayana might reply, that whole is the world not of essence but of existence, the world of facts. But he could only reply thus if he forget that the world of existence is, for him, as devoid of necessary connections as the world of essence. And he would never forget this; for he has the surest possible grasp on the rules of his own game. He would, I think, prefer to say that my description of thought is mere mythology – a romantic fiction, like those other romantic fictions called mathematics, science and philosophy. And that would be to concede my point: which is, that the logic of his position involves him in a wholesale denial of knowledge as such.

To push the criticism home and show that Mr Santayana's theory destroys itself, though I do not think it would be difficult, would take more space than I can here claim. But the moral is, I think, that his theory involves a false step; and I would identify this in the passage where he denies that essences are abstractions. They *are* abstractions, for all he says to the contrary; and the reason why he says they are not abstractions is just that they are *false* abstractions; that is, abstractions mistaken for something concrete. He is right to say that they are not the qualities of things taken in abstraction from the things, because, as he rightly says, there are essences which are nowhere embodied in things. They seem to me to be abstractions from *propositions* – the predicates of propositions, whether affirmative or negative propositions, treated as having a real being apart from the proposition or the act of propounding it. And, therefore, I cannot but accuse Mr Santayana of a crime which, in his own eyes, is especially heinous – the crime of crude psychologism, of being deceived in ones's philosophizing by mere forms of language. I do not think that is a very serious crime;

it happens to everybody. The real fault, I think, lies in his conception of what a philosophy should be. For him, it is a jewel: a thing to be polished and rounded and perfected and then offered to the world as one of a potentially infinite number of systems, all valid and all legitimate, because each has achieved a genuine intuition of an essence. That is a good description of a poem; it is a bad description of a philosophy, because a self-contradictory one. It involves maintaining (a) that any philosophy is as true as any other; (b) that the philosophy which holds that any philosophy is as true as any other is absolutely true, and any other absolutely false. In a word, it is a dogmatism clothed in the woolly garb of sceptical innocence. Whatever philosophy ought to be, I do not think it ought to be that.

DRAWINGS OF CONTEMPORARY PHILOSOPHERS BY R. G. COLLINGWOOD

R. G. Collingwood: Recent Publications

Compiled by
SUSAN DANIEL
Western Oregon University*

Bevir, Mark. "Universality and Particularity in the Philosophy of E. B. Bax and R. G. Collingwood." *History of the Human Sciences.* 12 no. 3 (1999): 55-69.

Blackburn, Simon W. "Reenactment as Critique of Logical Analysis: Wittgensteinian Themes in Collingwood." *Empathy and Agency.* Edited by Hans H. Kogler. Boulder: Westview Press, 2000.

Boucher, David. 'Tocqueville, Collingwood, history and extending the moral community', *British Journal of Politics and International Relations*, vol. 2, no. 3 (2000).

Boucher, David and Bruce Haddock, editors. *Collingwood Studies: Idealist Contexts.* Wales: Dinefwr Press, 1999.

Buda, Stanislaw. "Between Philosophy and History." *Kwartalnik-Filozoficzny* 26 no. 2 (1998): 187-205.

Carroll, Noel. *A Philosophy of Mass Art.* Oxford: Clarendon Press, 1998.

Collingwood, R. G. "Christianity in *Partibus*." Compiled and introduced by James Connelly and Peter Johnson. *Collingwood Studies* 6 (1999): 166-71.

_____. "Further Letters of R. G. Collingwood: Occasional Series No. 1." Compiled by Peter Johnson. *Collingwood Studies* 6 (1999): 175-89.

Connelly, James and A. Costall. "R. G. Collingwood and the Idea of a Historical Psychology." *Theory and Psychology* 10 no. 2 (2000): 147-70.

* Notification of additional items would be welcome. Please send to Dr Susan Daniel, Philosophy and Religious Studies Department, Division of Humanities, Western Oregon University, Monmouth, OR 97361, USA, OR daniels@wou.edu

Daniel, Susan. Review of *The Correspondence of R. G. Collingwood: An Illustrated Guide*, by Peter Johnson. *Collingwood Studies* 6 (1999): 190-91.

Diffey, T. J. "Some Thoughts on the Relationship between Gadamer and Collingwood." *Philosophical Inquiry* 20 nos.3-4 (1998): 1-12.

_____. "Arguing about the Environment." *British Journal of Aesthetics*. 40 no. 1 (2000): 133-48.

D'Oro, Giuseppina. "How Kantian is Collingwood's Metaphysics of Experience?" *Collingwood Studies* 6 (1999): 29-52.

_____. "Collingwood on Re-Enactment and the Identity of Thought." *Journal of the History of Philosophy* 38 no. 1 (2000): 87-101.

Gracia, Jorge J. E. *Metaphysics and Its Task: The Search for the Categorical Foundation of Knowledge*. Albany: SUNY Press, 1999.

Martin, Rex. "Action Explanations as Understanding Explanations." *Actions, Norms, Values*. Edited by Georg Meggle. Berlin and New York: de-Gruyter, 1999.

Oldroyd, D. "Non-written Sources in the Study of the History of Geology: Pros and Cons, in the Light of the Views of Collingwood and Foucault." *Annals of Science* 56 no. 4 (1999): 395-415.

Parker, Christopher. *The English Idea of History from Coleridge to Collingwood*. Andershot, England; Brookfield, Vermont: Ashgate, 2000.

Passmore, John. "Evidence for the Past." *History and Theory*. 38 no. 1 (1999): 132-39.

Peters, Rik. "Collingwood's Logic of Question and Answer, its Relation to Absolute Presuppositions: Another Brief History." *Collingwood Studies* 6 (1999): 1-28.

Ridley, Aaron. "Collingwood's Commitments: A Reply to Hausman and Dilworth." *Journal of Aesthetics and Art Criticism* 56 no. 4 (1998): 396-98.

Singer, Marcus G. "Presuppositions of Inference." *Pragmatism, Reason, and Norms: A Realistic Assessment*. Edited by Kenneth R. Westphal. New York: Fordham University Press, 1998.

Skeats, T. C. Review of *R. G. Collingwood*, by Aaron Ridley. *Library Journal* 124 no. 18 (1999): 86.

Twining, W. "R. G. Collingwood's *Autobiography*: One Reader's Response." *Journal of Law and Society* 25 no. 4 (1998): 603-20.

Vanheeswijck, Guido. "R. G. Collingwood and A. N. Whitehead on Metaphysics, History, and Cosmology." *Process Studies* 27 nos. 3-4 (1998): 215-36.

Wisner, David A. "Modes of Visualisation in Neo-Idealist Theories of the Historical Imagination: Cassirer, Collingwood, Huizinga." *Collingwood Studies* 6 (1999): 53-84.

BRITISH IDEALISM

T. H. Green and Justifying Human Rights[1]

Maria Dimova-Cookson
University College, London

One of the dilemmas which contemporary political theories of human rights face is whether, in view of the cultural diversity we live in, we can speak of universal human rights or not.[2] What is at stake is not trivial – on the one side political theory should face up to its task of explaining, and indeed, defending human rights. On the other hand it should remain sensitive to cultural difference, and many believe that this sensitivity is jeopardised by universalist accounts of human nature. Knowing that T. H. Green is a nineteenth century idealist, exponent of the idea of the common good, one can only assume that he would be among those philosophers that are categorised as foundationalist. However, Green's critique of the concept of 'natural rights' and his specific theory about how 'rights are made by recognition' define his account of human rights as sensitive to cultural diversity and historical context.[3] We could say, with a dosage of irony, that Green was a nineteenth century postmodernist. He argued that the concepts of 'natural rights' and 'laws of nature' are abstract, presumptuous and oblivious to the actual social practice in which rights occur. He spoke about 'consciousness of utility' and 'reference to acknowledged social good'.[4] Instead of defining human rights solely on the basis of analysis of human nature in the style of Locke and Rousseau, Green directs our attention to the social practice within which rights arise. My purpose in this paper, however, is not to emphasise this metaphysically lighter side of T. H. Green which could be fitted more easily in the environment of contemporary political theory. My aim is to demonstrate that the issue of human rights is such that it brings with itself dilemmas that can only be partially resolved and that Green's philosophy brings us at the heart of these dilemmas. Are individuals entitled to human rights on the strength of their rational nature or do they possess them on the grounds of belonging to a community that respects human rights? Can we give a fundamental justification of human rights or shall we take each case as it comes? Universal *versus* contingent, theory *versus* practice, individual *versus* society: these dilemmas are inherent to the issue of rights. Green occupies an interesting location between these poles because in his overall philosophy he develops two distinguishable approaches to justifying rights.

This paper pursues two objectives: to offer a new angle on Green's rights theory and to explore further the issues raised in it. The new angle is a result of juxtaposing Green's political theory on the one side and his moral philosophy on the other. The argument is that Green unwittingly develops two different justifications of human rights. His theory of rights leads us to a dilemma that begs some kind of resolution. The analysis of Green leads us to the discussion of the issue of justification and morality in general.

Green's theory of political obligation together with his moral philosophy in general leave us in doubt about the kind of justification he develops of human rights. I argue that he gives us two justifying theories, which although not fully contradictory to each other, are nonetheless different. In his political theory as presented on his *Lectures on the Principles of Political Obligation* (hereafter *Principles*) he argues that rights are based on social recognition linked to recognisable utility. In his moral theory familiar to us from *Prolegomena to Ethics* (hereafter *Prolegomena*), he argues that the ultimate purpose of social progress is the well-being of the individual. Peter Nicholson has pointed out to me that instead of holding this difference against Green, I should underline that Green's theory covers more than a single perspective. Believing in the advantages of versatility I narrow my criticism to the fact that Green should have been aware that these are related, yet different perspectives. Indeed, because his philosophy somehow embraces the two sides of a dilemma that remains such even nowadays, Green's theory of rights is particularly interesting.

Green's overall philosophy poses a dilemma. On what grounds are individuals entitled to rights? On the grounds of their special nature as human beings or on the grounds of social recognition? In the course of this paper we will see that this dilemma concerns the role of the individual in society:

should she be seen as the ultimate justification of any effort after social improvement, or as a contributor to the social well-being? Green's two philosophical approaches on justifying rights converge into the idea that rights are based on human moral nature. However, this leads us to see that morality has two aspects and we have to separate them if we are to offer a non-contradictory justification of rights. We are left facing the question how do we define the moral agent: as someone who needs respect and human treatment or as some who is capable of pursuing a project in a self-disinterested manner? Green would argue that these two alternatives are opposed only on the surface while in essence they are the two aspects of the same thing. However, when it comes to justifying rights, these two sides fall apart. I can be in a position where I am not involved in any positive moral action, yet I am still a moral agent. Am I entitled to rights then? This issue will be discussed in section three of this paper.

The paper takes the following strategy. The first section explains Green's rights theory by focusing on the concept of social recognition. We shall see that the idea of social recognition embraces both considerations about social practice and the nature of moral action. Section two presents briefly Green's ideas of human agency and morality as developed in the *Prolegomena*. It explains how, on the basis of these ideas, we can extract a different justificatory theory of rights. Section three engages with the questions Green lead us to and offers some solutions.

1. SOCIAL RECOGNITION AS THE FIRST PHILOSOPHICAL LINE OF JUSTIFYING RIGHTS

In a nutshell, in the *Principles* Green expounds the philosophy of social recognition, while in the *Prolegomena*, at least in part, he expounds the philosophy of the personal character of the moral ideal.[5] Let me start with the first.

Green's theory of rights rests on his concept of social recognition. Green argues against the idea of natural rights as he does not believe that we can speak about the individual in a meaningful way without taking into account her social environment. He claims that rights exist to the extent that they are recognised by society. This claim raises the obvious objection. Does it mean that if a society does not recognise any rights, the individual is not entitled to such? Green's defenders point out that his concept of social recognition is a complex one and it accounts not only for the explicit social recognition but also for implicit forms of agreement.[6] Tyler argues that the emphasis on social recognition of rights 'is a necessary aspect of the ontology, not just the epistemology of rights'.[7] The concept 'social recognition' sums up a whole theory. Green starts with observations about the practicalities of enacting rights but he continues to draw out the metaphysical contents of the meaning of 'recognition'.

The complexity of the concept of 'social recognition' is also underlined by the fact that Green uses the word 'recognition' with two different semantic connotations. The first usage is related to the practical social recognition and bears the meaning of 'agreeing on', 'consenting to'. The second usage is related to the metaphysical social recognition and describes the process of 'self-overcoming'. This dual usage results from the fact that Green refers to 'recognition' as an ordinary habitual action, on the one side, and as a moral action, on the other.

1.1. THE PRACTICAL ASPECT OF SOCIAL RECOGNITION

Green's insistence on the importance of social recognition with respect to rights is related to his desire to account for the practical procedure through which rights come into existence. The role of society with respect to the practical implementation of rights looms large. The individual is the agent who acts morally, yet society is 'the agent' who gives rights.[8] It is because Green is predominantly concerned with the question 'How do rights come into existence?' that his definition of rights is so heavily loaded with arguments about social recognition. Green's notion of the practical social recognition of rights is very complex because he wants to imbue it with metaphysical meanings. This notion contains within itself a theory of society, of public consciousness and of the state. I will explain the notion of practical social recognition by following his train of thought. The first stage is the realisation that rights *are given* to the individual by the society. The second is the assessment of the practical implications which follow from that.

Rights are powers which are given to the individual by her fellow human beings. One enjoys rights only so far as these are guaranteed and protected by society. How is that possible? In what fashion does society guarantee rights? Or, more precisely, how does society act unanimously? The existence of rights implies a social agreement as to which are the particular powers that should be recognised as rights, and as to the fact that all should act unanimously in guaranteeing these rights. If some recognise my rights but others violate them, I do not have proper rights. In the exercise of my rights, I and society act as partners. I carry the powers which can be exercised as rights, while society recognises them as rights, guarantees and protects them. As 'the others' are my partner, they have to act out of a 'common consciousness' and out of a 'common will'. This is the most difficult step towards introducing rights into practice: having society work as a whole, as a unit; building a society which unanimously shares the value of the individual's well-being. One of the arguments which Green develops is that society will recognise the individual's rights if there is, thereby, some obvious benefit for society as a whole. There should be some agreeable reason why the individual should have his powers guaranteed to him. While explaining the grounds on which rights unrecognised by the state should be so recognised, Green claims:

> The assertion by the citizen of any right, however, which the state does not recognise must be founded on a reference to an *acknowledged* social good . . . The reason that an assertion of an illegal right must be founded on reference to *acknowledged* social good is that, as we have seen, no exercise of a power, however abstractly desirable for the promotion of human good it might be, can be claimed as a right unless there is some consciousness of utility shared by the person making the claim and those on whom it is made.[9]

Here Green argues that the process of social recognition demands that the individual exercises the powers he claims as rights for the benefit of society. Green advances the idea that rights come to exist as a result of a long process of social interaction during which 'some consciousness of utility shared' by all is being created. It is only on the basis of this 'public consciousness' that rights can come into practice.[10]

Green makes it very clear that he is speaking about the practical process which leads to the introduction of rights; not about what ought to be the case, but what is the case in the actual practice. He himself immediately continues to say that '[i]t is not a question whether or not it [the asserted illegal right] ought to be claimed as right; it simply can *not* be except on this condition'.[11] Nonetheless, he does not view this practical process as unjust, or inhumane. He sees its logic and tries to explain it in terms which make it acceptable. Green's explanation is as follows. It is true that reality is full of examples of states where the abuse of human rights is part of the official legislation, the most obvious case being that of slavery. However, even if the state refuses to recognise rights which we may consider basic, there still exist smaller societies within the state which do recognise these rights. In the case of slavery, there always exists some minimal community of relatives or fellow-slaves amongst whom each slave is treated as a human being. 'The slave thus derives from his social relations a real right which the law of the state refuses to admit.'[12] This small society is the basis on which a social movement for slave rights can rest. The slaves will have their rights properly observed – that is, they will break free from slavery – when this society grows in numbers. Without a minimal society sharing a common consciousness of human respect towards each individual slave, the cause of slave rights is a non-starter.

Now we can better understand the practical side of Green's concept of social recognition. Green's emphasis is not so much on the 'recognition' but on the formation of a social consciousness. What Green wants to explain is that without the existence of public consciousness we are as far from rights as we can be. His opponents are those who believe that rights are 'natural', that rights belong to the individual regardless of their recognition by the rest. To these opponents Green wants to explain that without 'the rest' there are no rights. Green defends the idea of 'recognition' in a very wide sense. Recognition of rights is part of the process which creates public consciousness. The latter can arise only within a practical interactive environment. A better term for Green to express the idea behind his concept of 'social recognition', would have been 'social participation'. The emphasis of Green's protest against natural rights theorists, as well as the weight of his own theory, lies on the fundamental role of 'common consciousness'[13] in the process of enacting human rights: 'We have already seen that a right against society, as such, is an impossibility; that every right is derived from some social relation; that a right against any group of associated men depends on association, as *isos kai homoios* [an equal], with them and with some other men.'[14]

Such an account of human rights we can easily define as sensitive to historical and cultural circumstances. Green understands rights as a dynamic entity that develops and strengthens in the process in which different communities integrate with each other.[15] In certain states people enjoy a wider range of rights than in others. Furthermore, making an inappropriate claim for a right in a society incapable of recognising it may lead to 'the dissolution of this or that form of civil combination . . . [and] to the disappearance of conditions under which any civil combination is possible'.[16] However, Green's theory that rights depend on social recognition does not lead to the conclusion that rights have a contingent nature. And this is because social recognition itself is not a contingent entity. It is not something that could either exist or not exist: it is a factor intrinsic to human nature.

1. 2. SOCIAL RECOGNITION AS A MORAL ACT

Usually political theorists who strongly oppose the concept of natural rights (like Bentham and Marx, for example) reject the idea of universal human rights in general. Green is not one of them. Rex Martin argues that although Green criticises Hobbes, Spinoza, Rousseau and Locke, he himself develops further the ideas which they invested in the concept of natural rights.[17] This is so because in his rights theory Green makes an analysis of the individual's social nature.

The terminology of social recognition represents one of Green's various attempts to explain the nature of moral action. Let me first remind you of his most famous explanation of morality – the theory of the common good. According to it, the individual perceives her own true good as something that is good for her and others in common. The theory of the common good points to the human capacity of suspending interest in one's own gratification for the sake of a good of a higher order, or in other words, for the sake of the social welfare. In another paper I have argued that the theory of the common good is in essence a way of defining moral behaviour because it shows how one can pursue a project in a self-disinterested manner.[18]

The case with 'social recognition' is very similar. Green claims that the individual develops her moral potential through the act of recognising the rights of her fellow human beings: 'There ought to be rights, because the moral personality – the capacity on the part of the individual for making a common good his own – ought to be developed; and it is developed through rights; i.e., *through the recognition by members of a society of powers in each other* contributory to a common good and the regulation of those powers by that recognition.'[19] The mutual recognition of each other's capacities is part of what morality is about. A moral act is constituted by the individual's determination to contribute to the good of others in the same manner in which he contributes to his own good. Recognising other's rights is a moral act as the agent acts on representation not of his own interest, but of the interest of his fellow human beings. The terminology of social recognition comes as an additional restatement of what constitutes a moral action.

Now we can see that Green uses the term 'recognition' in at least two semantically different ways. One of the usages aims to emphasise the importance of social practice (social interaction) for the existence of rights. The other usage is in the sense of 'acting morally'. I recognise your claims for exercising your capacities freely; I treat you as an end; I treat you as an equal – for Green all these statements imply the same thing: I am acting as a moral agent. The ambiguity in the use of the term 'recognition' reflects the two levels on which Green employs the idea of social recognition: the more practical and the more philosophical one.

The function of the practical social recognition, as I have already argued in section 1.1, is in the process of forming a unanimous community where people share the same values and treat each other as equals, that is, as subjects of rights. Recognising each other's claims to exercise certain powers ('that spontaneous recognition by each of the claims of all others')[20] leads to developing common values. Green refers to the act of recognising as to an act of agreeing, consenting, conceding to the same thing. By acknowledging, agreeing on, recognising the same thing as important, we are building a common consciousness:

There can be no reciprocal claim on the part of a man and an animal each to exercise his powers unimpeded by the other, because there is no consciousness common to them. But a claim founded on such a common consciousness is already a claim *conceded*; already a claim to which reality is given by social recognition, and thus implicitly a right.[21]

Here Green uses 'social recognition' in the sense of agreement reached by interaction; in the sense of interaction out of which common consciousness has emerged. The fact that Green refers to people's recognition as to their ability to understand, is well revealed by the emphasis he places on the dependence of rights on the particular historical context. Any right an individual would claim, however 'desirable in an ideal state of things',[22] has to correspond to some existing public interest; it has to be 'recognisable', 'conceivable' to some minimal circle of people, who will, in their turn, guarantee this right.

What are the philosophical conclusions that can be drawn from Green's defence of social recognition? Clearly Green did not believe that what the case is is what the case ought to be, i.e., that we should accept states where human rights are not recognised as legitimate. Green's point, however, is that human rights come into existence by being practised in smaller communities and their exercise grows with the expansion of the number of the people who treat each other as equals. Belonging to some community is the only way of becoming a member of a larger community.[23] You can have your rights recognised by everybody only if you have them recognised by some, to start with. This is because the practice of rights is based on 'that common human consciousness which is evinced both by language . . . and by actual social relations'.[24] There is an essential element of trust and reciprocity: we trust the others that they share the same moral principles as us, and they will voluntarily fulfil their duties towards us in the manner in which we have done the same for them. We do not endow animals with rights precisely because they are unable the share with us the same attitude towards principles.[25] The idea here is that the exercise of human rights and, which is the same, human moral nature emerge and grow within a social environment. Rights are justified in the fact that we are moral agents, that we have consciousness of a common good and we are capable of overcoming our selfish impulses for principles we share with the others. 'A right is a power . . . secured to an individual by the community, on the supposition that its exercise contributes to the good of the community.'[26]

By explaining the nature of moral action through the terminology of social recognition, Green, I would argue, overemphasises the role of society with respect to the moral nature of the individual. The philosophical conclusions that can be drawn on the basis of his rights theory are that the essence of humanity and morality are to be found in the individual's contribution to a social welfare. If, as it is according to Green, one can claim rights only provided that there is some 'utility shared by the person making the claim and those on whom it is made', then one's entitlement to rights rests fully on how useful one can make herself to the others.

2. GREEN'S IDEAS OF HUMAN AGENCY AND MORALITY IN *PROLEGOMENA*: THE SECOND PHILOSOPHICAL LINE OF JUSTIFYING RIGHTS

What is lacking in the *Principles* and is very clearly present in the *Prolegomena* is the emphasis on the inner aspiration towards self-fulfilment. Green argued that only self-perfection can bring true self-satisfaction to an individual. The moral ideal was first defined as the pursuit of perfection (in Chapter I of Book III of the *Prolegomena*), and only subsequently (in Chapter III of Book III), as the pursuit of the common good. Green dedicated the better half of Chapter II (Book III) explaining '*The Personal Character of the Moral Ideal*'.[27] The moral ideal was presented as personal in at least two aspects. First in the sense that a person is the home of human spirit:

> [t]he human spirit cannot develop itself according to its idea except in self-conscious subjects . . . The spiritual progress of mankind is thus an unmeaning phrase, unless it means a progress *of* personal character and *to* personal character – a progress of which feeling, thinking, and willing subjects are the agents and sustainers, and of which each step is a fuller realisation of the capacities of such subjects.[28]

Secondly, the moral ideal has a personal character in the sense that the human individual should be regarded not a means but as the goal of social progress. 'To speak of any progress or improvement or development of a nation or society or mankind, except as relative to some greater worth of persons, is to use words without a meaning.'[29]

How can Green's theory of human agency be related to a theory of human rights? Through little additional reasoning. According to Green's theory, human nature is such that the individual needs to develop in order to achieve her full potential; she can always be more than what she is now. However, in order to achieve her self-fulfilment, a person needs to exercise and develop her capacities. This ever increasing potential for self-fulfilment goes hand in hand with an ever increasing vulnerability.[30] As every further self-fulfilment brings more self-satisfaction, the denial of a possibility for self-development causes suffering. If a person is essentially characterised by her permanent potential for improvement, the lack of such improvement undermines her nature as a human being.

On the basis of Green's philosophy we can reach the conclusion that we are entitled to rights because of the moral character of our needs. Because human nature implies capacity for moral agency, human needs are also moral needs. We should have rights because if we do not have them we cannot realise our humanity. The notions of moral need and moral vulnerability are implicit both in Green's theory of moral agency, and in his assertion of the absolute value of the individual.

We can see why, in view of Green's defence of the personal character of the moral ideal, one can find his critique of natural rights puzzling. One would expect that Green should argue that an individual is entitled to rights because of his nature as an agent who permanently pursues a vision of his better self.[31] We have also seen, however, that Green has good reason to criticise the idea of natural rights. He believes that a political theorist should account for the role of society, not only for the formation of rights, but for the formation of human personality. Without that he will end up with a false metaphysical picture of the individual. Green wants to explain that human 'nature' is social. Further to that, Green wants to equate the notion of morality with the social nature of the human individual. He rejects the concept of natural rights because it implies an antagonistic relation between the individual and society. Green concedes that there may be a conflict between the individual and the state, yet not between her and her fellow human beings. He says that rights may be ' "natural" in the sense of being independent of, and in conflict with, the laws of the state in which he lives, but they are not independent of social relations'.[32]

However, in his political theory, Green goes a bit too far along the road of asserting the link between the individual's self-fulfilment and her involvement in societal life. In essence, he identifies the individual with her social role. He is justified in arguing that such antagonism between the individual and society should not be assumed, yet he is wrong in ruling it out as a possibility. Such antagonism is possible when someone is uprooted from his own environment and forced to live in exile, among people of whose society he has not been a member. There are other possible scenarios where a person may find herself 'detached' from her immediate sur-rounding. Typical is Green's own example of the social reformer, whose 'very essence . . . consists in his being the corrector and not the exponent of the common feeling of his day'.[33] What is it, according to Green, that gives the social reformer the confidence that he is pursuing the right cause, regardless of any lack of public support? 'The breath of his life,' Green claims, 'is inspired from above, not drawn up from below. Those flashes of religious enlightenment which from time to time break on the slumbers of mankind often resemble in their history the discovery of scientific truth.'[34] The insight carried by the social reformer is how we, in the particular circumstances we live, as a society can lead a good life. And explaining what a good life is is one of Green's philosophical achievements in *Prolegomena*. The absolute good for Green is human perfection: 'the object generally sought as good [must be] a state of mind or character of which the attainment, or approach to attainment, by each is itself a contribution to its attainment by every one else'.[35] There he also claims that 'it is only so far as this development and direction of personality [to contribute to human perfection] is obtained for all who are capable of it (as presumably everyone who says 'I' is capable), that human society, either in its widest comprehension or in any of its particular groups, can be held to fulfil its function, to realise its idea as it is in God.'[36]

Although Green believes that human rights have a historical character, he does not doubt for a moment that our moral agency is 'ahistorical'. There had been no form of humanity preceding the stage whereby human beings were capable of regarding their fellow human beings' good as equal to their own. The capacity to endorse other people's good as part of one's own idea of good is the very essence of humanity: 'We may take it, then, as an ultimate fact of human history – a fact without which there would be no such history, and which is not in turn deducible from any other history – that out of sympathies of animal origin, through their presence in a self-conscious soul, there arise interests as of a person in persons.'[37] The human ability to pursue self-fulfilment in a self-conscious and 'self-distancing' way is ahistorical. The very contents of a moral ideal may develop throughout human history,[38] but not the fact that human beings have the capacity to further their own well-being by pursuing moral ideals.

3. RIGHTS AS EXPRESSION OF NEGATIVE FREEDOM; NEGATIVE AND POSITIVE MORALITY

The two philosophical lines of justifying rights converged into the claim that the philosophical grounds of human rights are to be found in the moral nature of the human agent. However, the ambiguity is now shifted to the issue how to define this moral nature. Green does say that '[t]here ought to be rights, because the moral personality – the capacity on the part of an individual for making a common good his own – ought to be developed; and it is developed through rights'.[39] Yet Green is ambiguous as to why moral personality should be developed. His rights theory, as we know it from the *Principles*, leaves the impression that people ought to be moral because, by being moral, they contribute to the common well-being. But in the *Prolegomena* Green implies that the reason for helping someone to become a moral agent is that this is part and parcel of developing his personality in general, of his achieving self-fulfilment and leading a full life. The ambiguity is the following: does morality consist in doing good for the others, and therefore, rest on social recognition, or does it consist in the personal effort of pursuing an ideal of perfection? Although these two aspects of the nature of morality are related, when it comes to the issue of human rights, they represent two different grounds for justifying rights.

Green gives us a clue as how to resolve this ambiguity. He claims that human rights are about 'the negative realisation' of one's powers. The way Green uses the terminology of positive and negative freedom has suggested to me the possibility of speaking respectively of positive and negative morality. In a statement which I shall quote shortly, Green speaks, in essence, about negative freedom. This statement is easily overlooked because he does not develop it further, and because he is generally thought of as the exponent of positive freedom. Green writes:

> Rights are what may be called the negative realisation of this power [the power of the individual freely to make the common good his own]. That is, they realise it in the sense of providing for its free exercise, of securing the treatment of one man by another as equally free with himself, but they do not realise it positively, because their possession does not imply that in any active way the individual makes a common good his own. The possession of them, however, is the condition of this positive realisation of the moral capacity . . . [40]

This statement throws light on how Green uses the terminology of 'negative' and 'positive' exercise of freedom. I have discussed elsewhere that the individual has negative freedom as a recipient, and positive freedom as an active agent.[41] Rights can be seen as a negative exercise of powers in the sense that the individual does what she does, thanks to the help of others; she uses her freedom as guaranteed to her, as given to her by the rest.

Green's use of 'negative' – 'positive' terminology in explaining the exercise of powers, as well as his practical and moral philosophy from *Prolegomena*, have led me to the observation that human morality is characterised not only by the goods one can actively produce, but also by what one needs. This terminology suggests a constructive way to describe better individual moral nature. We can speak *of positive and negative human morality* in order to account simultaneously for the fact that one may act in a self-disinterested way, on the one hand, and that one needs to be a recipient of self-disinterested action, on the other. Once we spell out fully the negative aspect of morality, we have clear grounds for the justification of rights: we are entitled to rights because we are negatively moral. As opposed to Green, whose concept of social recognition leads to the conclusion that rights are justified through positive morality, I claim that the metaphysical grounds of rights are to be found in negative morality.

4. CONCLUSION: RECONCILING THE TWO LINES OF THOUGHT IN GREEN'S PHILOSOPHY

Green's two philosophical lines of justifying rights converged in the idea that human moral nature is the ultimate ground of rights. However, what became obvious is that these two lines lead to the assertion of two separable sides of moral nature. So the paper started with the dilemma 'universalism versus cultural context' and ended with a discussion about two ways in which we can understand the connection between the individual and society, or what amounts to the same, the two ways in which we can understand human moral nature.

In summary I can say that in his overall philosophy Green analyses human practice from two separate perspectives, thus asserting two different conclusions. One of these perspectives, as developed in Green's political theory, and specifically, in his rights theory, focuses on the process of social interaction and draws conclusions about the fundamentally social nature of human experience. The other perspective, as developed in Green's moral philosophy, focuses on the work of the spiritual principle that is always enacted in the individual's personal experience. There Green argues against the idea of any 'impersonal Humanity' and that all things acquire their meaning and value only within a personal context.[42] If we are to give a final account of Green's theory of rights we have to deal with this dilemma: does Green believe that rights have a historical character (that is, they are metaphysically dependent on what the public consciousness is prepared to recognise), or does he have a concept of human individuality which justifies rights in a universal way (that is, we are moral by nature and thus are unconditionally entitled to rights)? As we have seen, this dilemma can be further expressed by a question about what constitutes human moral nature. Where does our moral nature reside: in our altruistic action expressed in active involvement in societal life, or in our personal sensitivity as human beings who are in a constant process of self-development and thus in constant need of exercising our personal capacities? In this paper I have argued that although in his political philosophy Green has committed himself to the former option, in his moral philosophy he has engaged himself with the latter.

The terminology of positive and negative morality which I have introduced reconciles two fundamental aspects of human nature: its fundamentally personal, and its fundamentally social, character. Our capacity for moral action and our need for moral treatment are two sides of the same coin. Delivering the message about the intrinsic social dimension of human individuality – which is Green's concern – should not be at the cost of abandoning his own theory of the personal embeddedness of the spiritual principle. It is true that our fulfilment always necessitates social context, yet it is always *a* human agent who is being fulfilled, and thus his fulfilment always bears his particular personal mark. The moral nature of the human character is not exhibited solely in the active commitment to others' good, but also in the need for moral action on behalf of the others.

Spelling out the fact that moral nature has a negative and a positive side bears important political implications in so far as there are always two possibilities as to how these two sides are going to co-habit with each other. It is possible that they can coexist in harmony, that is, that a person consumes moral resources but she also provides such for the others in return. However, there exists the possibility of a conflict where she needs moral treatment but does not necessarily offer such herself. A political theorist needs to be able to offer solutions, should this conflict occur. Green's theory of human rights does not address the problem in a straightforward manner, but his philosophy provides resources for resolving the question 'Is one entitled to rights when the public consciousness of one's fellow human beings does not recognise such rights?'

NOTES

1 I am mostly indebted to Peter Nicholson and Susan Mendus who have read drafts of this paper and given me substantial comments. Some of the ideas of this paper are also presented in Chapter 5 of a forthcoming book *T. H. Green's Moral and Political Philosophy: A Phenomenological Perspective*, Palgrave Press.

2 See Susan Mendus 'Human Rights in Political Theory' in *Political Studies*, 43 (1995), 10-24.

3 T. H.Green in *Lectures on the Principles of Political Obligation* in *Lectures on the Principles of Political Obligation and Other Writings*, ed. Paul Harris and John Morrow (Cambridge: Cambridge University Press, 1986). Hereafter, *Principles*; in quoting, the first figure will refer to the number of the page, the second, to the number of the section. *Principles*, 106, 136.

4 See *Principles*, section 52 on p. 46; the quotes are from *Principles*, 113, 143; 112, 143.

5 See Book III, chapter II of *Prolegomena*.

6 Nicholson speaks of '*implicit* social recognition' and of claims 'fully and *explicitly* recognised as legal rights'. Nicholson, *The Political Philosophy of the British Idealists*, (Cambridge: Cambridge University Press, 1990), 89, emphasis added. See also Geoffrey Thomas who argues that 'It is analysis that is needed, however, not impressionistic reaction'. Thomas, *The Moral Philosophy of T. H. Green* (Oxford: Clarendon Press, 1987), 351-6, 352.

7 Colin Tyler, *Thomas Hill Green (1836-1882) and the Philosophical Foundations of Politics* (Lampeter, Mellen, 1997), 179. Tyler writes this in reply to Thomas who argues that Green's 'moral epistemology' diverges from his 'moral ontology'. Thomas, *The Moral Philosophy of T. H. Green*, 351-6.

8 See *Principles*, section 139, 108.

9 *Principles*, 112, 143.

10 *Principles*, 113, 143.

11 *Principles*, 112, 143.

12 *Principles*, 109, 140.

13 *Principles*, 108, 139.

14 *Principles*, 110, 141.

15 This how Green understands the function of the state – as an institution that balances an adjusts the claims of different societies: '. . . the state being for its members the society of societies – the society in which all their claims upon each other are mutually adjusted'. *Principles*, 110, 141.

16 *Principles*, 116, 147.

17 See Rex Martin, 'Green on Natural Rights in Hobbes, Spinoza and Locke', in *The Philosophy of T. H. Green*, ed. Andrew Vincent (Aldershot: Gower Publishing Company, Ltd., 1986) 104-26.

18 'T. H. Green's Theory of the Common Good', *Collingwood Studies* vol. VI (1999), 85-109.

19 *Principles*, 26-7, 26, emphasis added.

20 *Principles*, 48, 55.

21 *Principles*, 108, 139, emphasis added.

22 *Principles*, 113, 143.

23 'Membership of any community is so far in principle membership of all communities as to constitute a right to be treated as a freeman by all other men, to be exempt from subjection to force except for prevention of force.' *Principles*, 109 and 140.

24 *Principles*, 109, 140.

25 'We cannot endow [an animal] with rights because there is no conception of a good common to him with us which we can treat as a motive to him to do to us as he would have us do to him.' *Principles*, 160, 208.

26 *Principles*, 159, 207

27 This is the title of Part A of Chapter II of Book III of the *Prolegomena*.

28 *Prolegomena*, 195, 185.

29 *Prolegomena*, 193, 184.

30 This is discussed in Chapter 2 of my *T. H. Green's Moral and Political Philosophy: A Phenomenological Perspective*, Palgrave Press, forthcoming.

31 See Book II of the *Prolegomena*.

32 *Principles*, 109, 140.

33 T. H. Green, 'The Force of Circumstances', *Works of Thomas Hill Green, Volume III*, ed. R. L. Nettleship (London: Longmans, Green, and Co, 1889), 3-10, 10.

34 *Works*, 10.

35 *Prolegomena*, 263, 245.
36 *Prolegomena*, 202, 191.
37 *Prolegomena*, 212, 201.
38 See Chapters IV and V of Book III of *Prolegomena*, entitled 'The Development of the Moral Ideal'.
39 *Principles*, 26, 26.
40 *Prolegomena*, 26, 25.
41 Chapter 4 of *T. H. Green's Moral and Political Philosophy: A Phenomenological Perspective*, Palgrave Press, forthcoming.
42 *Prolegomena*, 190, 181.

'THIS DANGEROUS DRUG OF VIOLENCE':
Making Sense of Bernard Bosanquet's Theory of Punishment[1]

COLIN TYLER
University of Hull

INTRODUCTION

The assumptions and goals of English penal policy changed markedly over the course of the Victorian era.[2] The shift which began in the 1820s towards the use of sentencing to moralise criminals through strict and severe punishment had effectively been replaced at the end of the century by a policy arising from a new understanding of England as 'a disabled society of ineffectual, devitalised, and overcontrolled individuals moulded [sic] by environmental and biological forces beyond their control.'[3] Penal policy had become less concerned with retribution and deterring the guilty, and more concerned with 'direct therapeutic intervention'.[4] Against this historical background, Bernard Bosanquet's writings on punishment, published in 1899 and 1918 respectively, may appear crude and reactionary.[5] He is at pains to counter the 'the growing repugnance to punishment', and seeks to restrain the 'revolt against the idea and practice' of it.[6] Often he has been portrayed as a strict retributivist, for whom punishment should be meted out to any responsible agent who deliberately violates the norms of the society in which she lives. If this characterisation of Bosanquet's position is accurate, then in historical context it seems that the 'dangerous drug of violence'[7] and repression had blinded Bosanquet to some of the most important subtleties of his contemporary society's ideology of fair punishment.

This is not simply an issue of historical importance. The current philosophical standing of Bosanquet's theory of punishment reflects the current standing of his political theory more generally. Ted Honderich's assessment is typical.[8] Self-consciously struggling to expound Hegel's theory, which he describes as being at least in part 'nonsense', Honderich writes in despair, 'Not a great deal of advantage can be had at this point by consulting the related views of the English Idealists. Bosanquet, for example, speaks of crime as having a bad effect on 'the general mind', which is not to be confused with even the collection of individual minds, mere 'atomic states of consciousness'.'[9] If, as Honderich alleges, Hegel's theory is 'of very secondary interest' to penal theorists,[10] then Bosanquet's derivative and correspondingly 'mystical' formulation is hardly worth noticing. Similarly, Alan Norrie argues that 'With the English Idealists, retributivism fell into careless hands.' He claims that Bosanquet surpassed in strength and depth even F. H. Bradley's advocacy of 'the totalitarian state', and presented a theory in which 'all notions of individual right were negated in favour of the organic unity of the [social] whole'.[11] Moreover, Norrie alleges that Bosanquet committed some very basic conceptual errors, for example with retributivism being 'defined as a collective social principle of vengeance'.[12] The British Idealists, and Bosanquet in particular, had created, in sum, a 'scrambled, decayed and inverted version of retributivism'.[13] The most developed and extended recent discussion of Bosanquet's theory of punishment is presented by Igor Primoratz.[14] Nevertheless, he too is highly critical, finally concluding that for all of Bosanquet's (alleged) attempts to argue otherwise, 'Bondage is bondage, not freedom.'[15]

Not all recent commentators have been so dismissive of Idealist theories. Hence, while still finding them confused and unconvincing, Frederick Rosen has noted that in fact Bosanquet was alive to the distinction between revenge and desert.[16] Nevertheless, by seeking to combine retribution, deterrence and reform in the ways that they did, Rosen argues that Bosanquet and the other Idealists such as T. H. Green, F. H. Bradley and J. M. E. McTaggart, presented a 'peculiar offspring of retributive theory.'[17]

One claim of this paper is that Honderich, Norrie, Primoratz and Rosen all fail to adopt Bosanquet's own philosophical perspective to a sufficient degree and all fail to appreciate sufficiently his wider intellectual context. Consequently, all of these critics underestimate the internal coherence and force of his theory. It is for this reason that they see Bosanquet's position as confused, particularly in its analysis of the relationship between retribution, deterrence and reform. It is with an examination of this alleged confusion that the present paper begins to make sense of Bosanquet's writings on punishment. Furthermore, the paper shows that Bosanquet's writings contain the roots of two penal theories which are of far greater contemporary relevance than the confused retributivism of which often he has been accused. These are the theories of punishment as social expression and as communication. In this way, I hope also to rectify the neglect and misunderstanding which this important area has suffered even in the writings of commentators who are sympathetic to other aspects of Bosanquet's social and political thought.[18]

RETRIBUTION, DETERRENCE AND REFORM

It has been claimed then – most forcefully by Fred Rosen – that the theories of punishment developed by Bosanquet and the other Idealists contain an uneasy mix of retribution, deterrence and reform. This curious blend is, for Rosen, in fact an essentially *ad hoc* and unstable compromise between competing justifications and ends of punishment, more a pragmatic public policy than a philosophical theory.

There is certainly something paradoxical about the relationship between reform, deterrence and retribution in Bosanquet's theory. For example, he is scathing in his rejection of reform as the basis of punishment in both *The Philosophical Theory of the State* and 'On the Growing Repugnance to Punishment'. In the former work, he states that,

> If the reformation theory is to be seriously distinguished from the other theories of punishment, it has a meaning which is unjust to the offender himself. It implies that his [the criminal's] offence is a merely natural evil, like disease, and can be cured by therapeutic treatment directed to removing its causes. But this is to treat him not as a human being; to treat him as a 'patient,' not as an agent; to exclude him from the general recognition that makes us men.[19]

Reform of the individual's deficient character is only appropriate as a goal of state action where the transgressor lacks a capacity for agency. However if she lacks the capacity for agency then she also lacks moral responsibility for her actions and so cannot be an object of punishment. If you are not an agent, then quite simply 'you are not a moral being'[20] meaning that you can be used and moulded for social purposes, rather than respected as a person. Nevertheless, Bosanquet wishes to retain some element of reform in his theory.[21]

Similarly, Bosanquet rejects the deterrence theory as a basis for punishment, this time on the grounds that it provides no bulwark against punishing the innocent in the service of a higher value, such as achieving the greatest aggregate happiness or self-realisation.[22] Bosanquet's rejection of deterrence is grounded, then, in his belief that it is a fundamental premise of our ideas of justified punishment that there must be some basis of guilt. Even so, he holds that, 'The graduation of punishment must be almost entirely determined by experience of their operation as deterrents.'[23]

In short, how does Bosanquet support the claim that: 'Deterrence and reformation are expansions, outgrowths of its [punishment's] central character [as] the negation of the evil will, and so long as the central character is secured, modifications of method are allowable in the interests of deterrence and reformation'?[24]

Bosanquet's position starts to look less peculiar and confused when one employs the heuristic device of viewing his theory through Herbert Hart's categories of (1) the definition of punishment, (2) the General Justifying Aim, and (3) the principle of distribution.[25]

1. THE DEFINITION OF PUNISHMENT

To understand Bosanquet's definition of punishment, one must begin by appreciating that even though the greatest philosophical debts of his penal theory are owed to Hegel, he is self-consciously writing against the background of Emile Durkheim's *De la Division du Travail Social*, which was first published in French in 1893, six years before the first edition of *The Philosophical Theory of the State*.[26] Durkheim analyses punishment as a 'social fact' – that is, as a relatively stable and empirically observable pattern of social behaviour.[27] Bosanquet recognises that Durkheim's sociological approach has the great benefit of identifying punishment as, 'essentially a reaction of passionate feeling, graduated in intensity, which society exerts through the mediation of an organised body over those of its members who have violated certain rules of conduct.'[28] Bosanquet notes that for Durkheim, in its most immediate form punishment 'is, in essence, simply the reaction of a strong and determinate collective sentiment against an act which offends it.'[29] Bosanquet adds immediately: 'It is idle to include such a reaction entirely under the head either of reformation, or of retaliation, or of prevention.' An analysis of the proper place of each of these elements can be carried out only once this initial stage of defining punishment has been passed.

Yet even allowing for Bosanquet's appreciation of and partial agreement with Durkheim, it remains the case that he could never be satisfied with his purely sociological analysis. The identification of each social fact draws 'every serious student of social matters' to consider the network of social practices of which that fact forms a part. This network exists at the level of 'mind' ensuring that sociology is at best a prelude to philosophy.[30]

One of the main deficiencies of Durkheim's analysis in Bosanquet's eyes is that it misconceives the place of morality and law in the constitution of a crime.[31] It is not simply that punishment is essentially a specific type of emotional response, as Durkheim argues that it is. The type of response which is (partially) constitutive of punishment must have a particular source: it must spring from a recognition of the violation of a publicly promulgated law: 'with less than this there is no true crime.'[32] Moreover, this response must be expressed through the enforcement of the law by a public body which is formally authorised to do so, such as a court.[33]

It can be seen from this analysis that Bosanquet recognises all five elements of Hart's definition of punishment.

'(i) It must involve pain or other consequences normally considered unpleasant.

'(ii) It must be for an offence against legal rules.

'(iii) It must be of an actual or supposed offender for his offence.

'(iv)   It must be intentionally administered by human beings other than the offender.

'(v)   It must be imposed and administered by an authority constituted by a legal system against which the offence is committed.'[34]

2. THE GENERAL JUSTIFYING AIM OF PUNISHMENT

The General Justifying Aim of Punishment (GJA) is the end or goal of punishment; that is, the circumstance or value which punishment seeks to bring about or to serve. For utilitarians such as Hart and Jeremy Bentham, the GJA is to secure the greatest aggregate happiness within the political community.[35] The GJA in Bosanquet's theory is the maintenance of the community's system of rights and obligations,[36] to the extent that that system facilitates the self-determination of the citizens both as individuals and as groups. The last subclause is vital. The system of rights and obligations is valid to the extent that it facilitates the self-determination of persons. This is a notoriously complex claim in Bosanquet's thought, and in this paper I do not have the opportunity to enter into the debate about its meaning. It is essential to note two points however. First the system *as a whole* must be sustained, even where this conflicts with the need to sustain any *particular* right or obligation[37] Second Bosanquet's Kantianism leads him to argue that the opportunity to subjectively will objectively valid goals is a necessary precondition of leading a worthwhile life. (This contention is returned to with the discussion of Bosanquet's social theory in the next section of this paper, 'The Expressivist Theory of Punishment'.)

3. THE PRINCIPLE OF DISTRIBUTION

Hart's third category – 'the principle of distribution' – constitutes in part an answer to 'the question of Distribution': 'To whom may punishment be applied [legitimately]?'[38] The one serious answer to this question in Hart's eyes is "Only to an offender for an offence'.[39] This principle has two main components. The 'liability' sub-principle of distribution relies upon the notion of guilt and is thereby retributive (harm is inflicted on the criminal because he has deliberately violated publicly-promulgated and enforced laws).[40] Hart's second sub-principle of distribution is the 'Amount' of punishment.[41] He considers three ways in which this aspect of the principle of distribution of punishment affects the proper amount of punishment. The first is via mitigation,[42] the second is via 'the somewhat hazy requirement that 'like cases be treated alike'', and the third is via the requirement of proportionality between the seriousness of the offence and the severity of resulting punishment.[43] Each of these three variables 'may qualify the pursuit of our General Aim and is not deducible from it.'[44] In short, the liability sub-principle is determined by considerations of retribution, and the amount sub-principle diminishes the quantity of punishment which would otherwise be authorised by the General Justifying Aim of punishment.

What can the principle of distribution show us in Bosanquet's theory? When Bosanquet states that the demand for punishment of a criminal who has violated social values 'is the demand of justice pure and simple',[45] he is making a claim about liability under the principle of distribution (that it should be retributive): he is not making the type of claim regarding the GJA of punishment which – in effect – his critics believe him to be making. The amount of punishment is more complex, particularly the third requirement of ensuring some degree of proportionality between the seriousness of the crime and the resulting punishment. Bosanquet regards the belief that there should be an equivalence between the offence and the punishment as a mere 'superstition'.[46] Certainly his Kantianism is evident in his belief that the seriousness of an offence is determined by a combination of the moral quality of the agent's motive, and the harm caused by the crime.[47] Unlike Kant however, Bosanquet believes that neither of these factors is amenable to accurate measurement.[48] This has at least two very significant consequences. First, instead of attempting to determine the appropriate quantity of punishment by referring to the level of the criminal's moral guilt, Bosanquet argues that 'The graduation of punishments must be almost entirely determined by experience of their operation as deterrents.'[49] Second, mitigation is impossible to calculate.[50]

Hopefully, Bosanquet's theory of punishment now looks somewhat more coherent and less authoritarian than critics allege. Punishment is by definition the emotional reaction of a community against a responsible person who has violated of legally promulgated norms and values, with this reaction being expressed through due legal process. Furthermore, punishment is only justified if it serves its legitimate General Justifying Aim; that is, if it serves to maintain a system of rights and obligations which facilitates the self-determination of the citizens. Finally, the inability to determine accurately the level of guilt entails that the amount of punishment must be determined by the imperative to realise the GJA through deterrence of future crime (primarily). The criminal is respected as a Kantian end in this process in that he is treated as a responsible being (through public trial for the violation of known laws),[51] thus legitimising his (partial) treatment as a means (through the determination of sentencing on the grounds of deterring future crimes).[52]

For all of our success here, one should not be too complacent. Certain key problems remain. First the link between personal self-determination and the socially established system of rights and obligations remains vague, especially where individuals judge that the former conflicts with the latter. Second it remains unclear whether Bosanquet can successfully reconcile punishment understood as therapeutic reform with the conceptual requirement that to be a criminal one must be responsible for one's actions. Bosanquet tries to solve these problems through his Hegelian theory of punishment as annulment, which forms the subject of the following two sections.

THE EXPRESSIVIST FUNCTION OF PUNISHMENT

The concept of annulment is central to Bosanquet's penal theory, even though its meaning is not immediately obvious from his writings. Yet some elements of it should be familiar from the previous sections of this paper. In 'On the Growing Repugnance', he writes, punishment 'is a negation of an evil will which has been realised in action; and is emphasised by a formal social deliberation and sentence, and some overt act which stamps the annulment on the person or belongings of the offender.'[53] Or again, 'This, I take it, and not the infliction of pain, is the essence of punishment. It is the formal verdict or censure of the social authority, marked by some overt act such as the dullest capacity cannot misread.'[54]

Ted Honderich objected to Hegel's concept of annulment – the 'negation of an evil will' – that 'To reproduce this doctrine more faithfully and intelligibly would require a considerable and tedious excursus into the philosophy of Absolute Idealism.'[55] Bosanquet himself believes that a Hegelian theory of annulment such as his own does not require a grandiose explanation (even though it is possible to give one if that is requested). Indeed he does not even present his theory in terms of annulment in *The Philosophical Theory of the State*. When he does refer to annulment, he is very low-key. Consider his explanation of 'the ground and nature of punishment' in 'On the Growing Repugnance to Punishment'.[56] He asks, 'How can you annul a fact or an act? There are many methods. You can pull down a building, break open a locked gate, cancel a deed, make a liar tell the truth and apologise. A resolution of the House of Commons can be expunged.'[57] To a annul something is, in other words, to abolish it, to neutralise the effect which it has produced in the world, and, in the case of the liar, to change that part of its nature which made it what it had been previously.

So how does Bosanquet believe one can annul a crime? To answer that question, it is necessary to sketch the main features of his social theory, which can be broken down into five key stages. While formulating these stages, it may be helpful to adopt two distinctions: 'ultimate values' are values which possess intrinsic worth, and 'principal values' are values which an individual or group holds to be 'ultimate values'.[58]

(1) *Bosanquet is a realist regarding ultimate values (which he sees as forming a system)*. In other words, Bosanquet believes that there exists a system of (in Brink's words) 'moral facts and moral properties whose existence and nature are independent of people's beliefs and attitudes about what is right or wrong.'[59] For brevity I shall call these realist ultimate values 'objective values'. The fact that objective values form a system is crucial here. There is no one objective value which orders other objective values, as there is for, say, Plato. Instead objective values form a harmonious and complete system, a system with reference to which everything else which possesses worth derives its significance (everything which has worth but is not an ultimate value).

(2) *An agent's life is valuable to the extent that, (i) it embodies a system of principal values which reproduces the one system of objective values, and (ii) does so through the agent's subjective will.*

(3) *The finite individual is unlikely to be able to reproduce perfectly this harmonious system in her life if she lives in isolation from a community or communities with which she identifies her self and identity deeply.*

(4) *Enriching communities constitute networks of values which embody principal values, and such communities offer the best opportunities for reproducing the system of objective values.*

(5) *The particular agent tends to increase the value of her personal life by integrating it – through her unconstrained choice – into the life of such communities.*

The basic intuition behind this theory is familiar enough. For a number of reasons, individuals can only plan and perform the vast bulk of their actions against a social background. The first and most straightforward reason is that certain types of action require, in a purely instrumental fashion, the cooperation of other persons. For example, one can only make a fortune on the stock market if other people conduct business with you, and if other people buy and sell the products on which the value of the shares depends. A *modus vivendi* and purely private goals are required in this case. Second, certain forms of action are only possible when people cooperate deliberately as a unit. For example, one can only be the lead violinist in an orchestra if other people play with you, and each of these people must conceive of themselves as engaging with you in the same type of musical activity. The goal is an 'inherent public good' in Raz's terminology.[60] Third, most of an agent's actions presuppose ways of conceptualising the world which are inherited from her social background. The agent has to be socialised into at least one epistemic and normative perspective (via her initiation into social practices) before she is able to perform any action self-consciously. Drawing on Charles Taylor's later formulation, each such perspective is constituted by the intersubjective 'set of common terms of reference' which is logically implied by the conceptual and linguistic structures of the discourse in which these social practices operate. This third category obtains for most if not all of the actions falling under the first two categories.[61]

It is in consequence of the fact than an agent's actions presuppose intersubjective concepts and values that the process of annulment logically requires social self-expression. In punishing the performance of a criminal act, the legal system formally reaffirms the principal values which on the one hand the act presupposes, and which on the other it has violated. Punishment re-expresses the social judgement that the violated norms are social values.

Clearly this move from intersubjectivity to annulment needs to be examined more closely here. It is revealing that Bosanquet expounds the notion of annulment through a discussion of precedent-setting.[62] He asks of an unconventional act, 'What must you do to prevent its becoming a precedent? There is only one way. You must annul the fact or act.'[63] Similarly, 'A bad [sc. criminal] act has come into being. It has so far established a vicious rule, a precedent hostile to the body or soul of the community.'[64] Punishment annuls that precedent in the following sense. The criminal's deliberate violation of a system of settled legally-recognised rights and obligations undermines the authoritative status of the values of his community. This is significant for two key reasons. First it makes it less likely that these rights and obligations will be honoured by the criminal and others in the future. Second it harms the self-understanding and coherence of the community.

The second of these reasons is the more significant for present purposes. The legal system of rights and obligations formally instantiates values which are fundamental to the community. 'Fundamental' values refers here to something the intersubjective meanings[65] which structure the community and give it its particular character. Punishment becomes important against this background in that it represents the reassertion of the community's loyalty to its most basic values. Punishment cancels the negative precedent set by the deliberate violation of the authoritative values by an agent whose determinate capacity for agency nevertheless presupposes (intersubjectively) an adherence to the violated system of values. This aspect of punishment represents a vital facet of its nature as an act of annulment: formal social condemnation cancels the negation of the authoritative status of the values which are instantiated by the established legal system of rights and obligations.[66]

Bosanquet cannot be a retributivist theorist in any straightforward sense given the role played by social condemnation within his theory. Alan Norrie and Hastings Rashdall go too far when they claim that 'his theory was not really retributive at all', and Rosen does not go far enough in his scepticism regarding the theory's retributive status.[67] In fact retribution occupies a central position within what is nevertheless an expressivist theory of punishment. Punishment operates as annulment when the remorse of the guilty criminal, as brought about through (i) the ceremony of a formal and public trial in which the accused person is fully respected as a responsible agent and (ii) hard treatment which reaffirms *to the community itself* the sacredness of the values which the criminal has violated and which the community holds as principal values. Retribution has a constitutive value then, arising out of its relationship to the maintenance of a system of rights and obligations, which is itself justified to the extent that it helps to secure the conditions in which citizens can realise their best lives. The peculiarity picked up on by Rosen (regarding the 'mix' of retribution, deterrence and reform) stems in part from the fact that this GJA – the maintenance of a legitimate system of rights – can also be achieved through non-retributive methods, such as policies of deterrence and reform. Nevertheless, retribution symbolises a core presupposition of punishment, which is that the criminal is at least in part a morally responsible rational agent. Without recognition of this responsibility, the community could not understand its own laws as possessing objective worth even when they have been or are being violated. Sir Walter Moberly captured the essence of this view well: 'In the face of its violation, they ['the powers that be'] are under moral obligation to do something to reassert the power and majesty of the law transgressed or to vindicate the cause betrayed.'[68]

Consider Bosanquet's position against the background of the analysis of one of the leading expressivists, Joel Feinberg.[69] Feinberg supports Henry M. Hart's claim that "crime' . . . is conduct which, if duly shown to have taken place, will incur a formal and solemn pronouncement of the moral condemnation of the community.'[70] Feinberg goes on to note that the expressivist position can draw on many justifications, including (i) *'Authoritative disavowal'* – punishment by the state which formally and publicly condemns the acts of one of its own functionaries, thereby simultaneously disavowing the actions of that individual and reaffirming its own fundamental ethical principles as the state;[71] (ii) *'Symbolic nonacquiescence'* –

punishment which expresses the community's condemnation of the violation of its principal values, thereby maintaining its own integrity as a moral entity;[72] (iii) *'Vindication of the law'* – the integrity of the law is confirmed in the punishing of acts which violate its imperatives; (iv) *'punitive damages'*;[73] (v) *'Absolution of others'* – the punishment of a particular person exonerates the other suspects.[74]

Bosanquet understands justified punishment as the second of Feinberg's forms of reprobation;[75] that is, as an act of symbolic nonacquiescence. 'The violation of right within the moral community has called forth a shudder of repudiation which is at the same time a reflex stroke and shock directed against the guilty person.'[76] The idea of repudiation goes to the heart of symbolic nonacquiescence: by punishing the criminal the community reaffirms its own adherence to its principal values. Specifically, punishment reaffirms the validity of a system of rights and obligations which the community (as it expresses itself through the legitimate acts of the judicial organs of the state) holds to be fundamental in the realisation of the best lives of its members. Counterfactually: to fail to punish a crime would be to fail to show the respect due to the system of rights and obligations, thereby undermining their authoritative status in the minds of law-abiding citizens.

This is the first of two stages of the argument that punishment is a process of annulment: formally expressed social condemnation of a deliberate violation of established laws cancels the disaffirmation of the society's legally embodied principal values while still showing respect for the criminal as a responsible agent. The society has asserted itself without belittling its wayward member, and in so doing has maintained its own integrity.

Thus far this explanation of Bosanquet's concept of annulment has concentrated solely on the punishers' attitudes to the annulling act of punishment. Yet there is another side to punishment and it is impossible to understand Bosanquet's theory correctly unless one takes account of this crucial aspect of his thought.

THE COMMUNICATIVE FUNCTION OF PUNISHMENT

The offender is a responsible person, belonging to a certain order which he recognises as entering him and as entered into by him, and he has made actual his intention hostile to this order . . . In other words, he has violated the system of rights which the State exists to maintain, and by which alone he and others are secured in the exercise of any capacity for good, this security consisting in their reciprocal respect for the system.[77]

Primoratz's response to this passage from the *Philosophical Theory of the State* is that it is unconvincing, for example, to say to a thief that in punishing him you are doing what he really wills.[78] He gives four possible responses from the thief, each of which he believes defeats Bosanquet's claim. The thief could be (1) an amoralist, (2) a utilitarian living in circumstances which justify theft on utilitarian grounds, (3) a Proudhonian anarchist, or (4) a philosophical anarchist.

To answer Primoratz it is necessary to understand precisely what Bosanquet means when he states in *The Philosophical Theory* that, in punishment, 'we are dealing with a question of social logic and not of empirical psychology.'[79] This is a controversial claim in its own right. Norrie is highly dismissive of it: 'Quite so. Thus the point of view of the individual is peremptorily discarded. Where the individual rejects the demands of the 'social logic', he is simply regarded as unfit for membership of the social organism'.[80] This claim has led many other liberals to fear the role of annulment in Bosanquet's penal theory. That 'The offender is a responsible person, belonging to a certain order which he recognises as entering into him and as entered into by him, and he has made actual an intention hostile to this order'[81] seems to have some very sinister implications. Bosanquet is undeniably making the claim that the criminal may not be conscious of the conditions necessary for his moral life, and therefore may violate laws deliberately, without realising that they embody imperatives which arise out of her underlying system of right. Allegedly this leads his theory of annulment to justify authoritarianism, and for certain critics it even justifies totalitarianism.

In reality, Bosanquet's position is far more liberal than Norrie and the other critics believe. The first point to make in response is that the attack fails to appreciate the necessary role of personal subjectivity in Bosanquet's theory of political obligation and thereby its role in his theory of law and punishment.[82] A valuable life must be (in part) a freely chosen (sc. subjectively and inherently affirmed) life for Bosanquet, and importantly it is a life which necessarily presupposes the exercise of (and hence the capacity for) moral agency. Bosanquet stands in the Kantian tradition, just as Hegel and Green do, with the consequence that moral agency presupposes that actions should be performed 'out of reverence for the [moral] law' – one must perform one's duty *'for the sake of duty'*.[83] This point is expressed in less Kantian terms and in the light of Bosanquet's value realism by the proposition that an act is moral to the extent that the agent's subjective will is inherently motivated to realise an objectively valuable goal.

Second, even though Bosanquet sees something positive in punishment in a civilised society,[84] he rejects explicitly the blind affirmation of every infliction of punishment which drives the allegation of totalitarianism. As he writes in 'On the Growing Repugnance',

> any decent community . . . on the whole equally maintains certain general rights. That in doing so it may defend a state of things which contains much injustice and needless inequality is very true, and may be a further condition which tends totally to discredit the idea of punishment. The remedy for this is to improve the social system; not to fetter the reactions of the social will for good.[85]

Bosanquet never argues that the maintenance of all social norms is intrinsically valuable, nor does he even believe this of a society's system of rights and obligations. The worth of established norms, rights and obligations is derived from the support which they give to the external conditions of individual self-determination.[86] In violating the legitimate norms and systems, the agent violates the intersubjective framework presupposed by her determinate capacity for agency, as well as other enabling frameworks of which she is probably more conscious.[87] In so doing she undermines her own capacity to act, although without consciously recognising the fact. It is in this sense that punishment becomes the agent's *right*. By annulling the action, therefore – by neutralising its power in the world – one is reaffirming the criminal's right to self-determination. This is what Bosanquet has in mind when he states unequivocally that, 'There is no true punishment except where one is an offender against a system of rights which he shares, and therefore [where he is an offender] against himself.'[88] Punishment forms part of 'the general recognition that makes us men.'[89]

It is not simply that society coerces the criminal through punishment to act against her will and to respect the law in the future. There is a communicative aspect to the process as well.

> Primarily, no doubt, chastisement by pain, and the appeal to fear and to submissiveness, is effective through our lower nature, and, in as far as operative, substitutes selfish motives for the will that wills the good, and so narrows its sphere. But there is more . . . [W]hen we kick against the pricks, and it reacts upon us in pain, this pain . . . brings us to our senses, as we say; that is, it suggests, more or less, a consciousness of what the habitual system means, and of what we have committed in offending against it.[90]

The communicative function of punishment is a source of much contemporary debate, particularly in the writings of R. A. Duff and Andrew von Hirsch. The debate has clear echoes of Bosanquet's theory.[91] For example, Duff has noted that:

> Punishment, like moral blame, respects and addresses the criminal as a rational moral agent: it seeks his understanding and his assent; it aims to bring him to repent his crime, and to reform himself, by communicating to him the reasons which justify our condemnation of his conduct. A system of criminal law and punishment can now be seen as a unitary enterprise of dialogue and judgment in which law-abiding citizens, defendants and convicted offenders are all called to participate.[92]

From this perspective, the agent should be respected as a person, as a being capable of making choices rationally, and of abiding by laws for moral reasons. The role of punishment is to express a judgement which appeals to the rational facilities of the agent; to make people obey because the law is legitimate, rather than because of the fear of suffering harm at the hands of the criminal justice system if they violate that law.

Von Hirsch makes the contrast with a purely deterrent (or 'neutral sanction') theory very well: 'A neutral sanction would treat offenders and potential offenders much as beasts in a circus, as creatures which must merely be conditioned, intimidated, or restrained.'[93]

There are important areas of disagreement between communicative theorists. Von Hirsch is sceptical, for example, about Duff's claim that hard treatment punishments can awaken the criminal's conscience in such a way as to bring the criminal to freely pay penance for violating her society's legal standards. For von Hirsch hard treatment is at best an adjunct to censure, and fulfils a deterrent function rather than a communicative one. Duff favours 'such [hard treatment] 'punishments in the community' as community service orders and probation',[94] rather than 'long prison sentence[s]' or fines.

Bosanquet recognises that what are now called hard treatment punishments are merely one mode of fostering the agent's best life. He states explicitly that in some cases the correct form of state action is non-penal prevention, such as the reform of social or economic institutions. For example, he advocates welfare reform rather than prison to remove the compulsion placed on the individual to steal food in a famine.[95] What must be remembered throughout is that, 'Punishment is to protect rights, not to encourage wrongs.'[96] On balance, he is drawn towards a position which is very similar to that adopted by Duff.

> You do not really know what punishment means till you have realised the case of the fraudulent company-promoter, the cruel parent, the unfaithful wife . . ., who have listened to what they did in secret, rehearsed in a public court before all Israel and the sun, and commented on by the weighty voice of the appointed social authority. *Some overt act is also necessary, some visible and sensible diminution of personality – imprisonment perhaps, or some deprivation of the children (which is practically a penalty, though primarily in the children's interest) – to make sure that the dullest capacity, including that of the guilty person if dimmed and hardened by sin, shall not fail to apprehend the intensity of the annulling act.*[97]

The tone of this passage may seem malevolent, and yet it should not be thought that Bosanquet is advocating the vitriolic application of hard treatment punishments. Throughout his discussions of punishment he reasserts his abhorrence of the abuses to which the penal system is subject.[98] Furthermore, he is emphatic that, 'It seems to me that as a general principle the [prison] regime should be at once strict in matters of comfort and constructive in matters of occupation.'[99] Finally he is explicit that one should apply the minimum level of punishment that is required to maintain the system of rights and obligations.[100] The position developed by Duff and Bosanquet is preferable to von Hirsch's more pessimistic attitude to the communicative potentials of certain forms of hard treatment, such as the misnamed process of 'mediation' between the criminal and the victim.[101]

A familiar difficulty arises at this point. Does Bosanquet's anticipation of the communicative theory mean that his theory justifies reform as a mode of punishment? It would be misleading to characterise repentance as reform. Censure aims to awake the criminal's conscience (for want of a better word), whereas reform has overtones of therapeutic treatment and hence, implies that the criminal is, as Bosanquet himself puts it, 'a patient' rather than 'an agent'.[102] 'It implies that his offence is a merely natural evil, like disease, and can be cured by therapeutic treatment directed to removing its causes.' Bosanquet is wrong to believe that reform can have any place in punishment. Broadmoor is a secure hospital, not a prison.

Even accepting that certain hard treatment punishments can have a communicative as well as an expressive aspect, a final question remains. What would Bosanquet say about the more extreme case where even after being punished the criminal's conscience does not bring him to regret his infraction? Which answer is appropriate here depends on the reason for the offender's lack of regret. If it is caused 'merely' by the agent's failure to appreciate the implicit logic and presuppositions of her will, then Bosanquet's basic theory remains intact, although the methods of censure may need to be rethought. The case is quite different however where the agent's lack of repentance is explained by the fact that he is an 'outlaw'. Alan Norrie makes a great deal of Bosanquet's assertion that, 'any sane man [who] fails altogether to recognise in any form the assertion of something which he normally respects in the law which punishes him . . . is outlawed by himself and the essentials of citizenship are not in him.'[103] Bosanquet's point is simply that there must be some form of recognition of the validity of the transgressed values in the structure of the criminal's actions for the infliction of pain to constitute an act of annulment.[104] This recognition could be implicit within her will (for example, through the intersubjective presuppositions of her actions) or explicit in her conscience (for example, through her grudging acceptance that she has done something morally wrong). By definition however, the outlaw 'fails to recognise in any form' the validity of the transgressed values, meaning that any infliction of pain on her cannot constitute an act of punishment *per se*.

This does not mean that any individual who is not a member of our community can be abused with impunity. In that we treat every individual with whom we have contact as a person at least to some degree – for example, by remonstrating with her or even by threatening her verbally – we implicitly recognise her as a rational, self-determining being. Whether we ourselves understand it or not, our actions presuppose this recognition because 'recognition is a matter of logic, working on and through experience, and not of choice and fancy.'[105] Consequently our interaction with the outlaw implies that she should be accorded certain basic rights and obligations. She should never be merely used; respect should be paid to her status as a person, as a being who is responsible for her own actions. She should be treated as an end in herself.

CONCLUSION

I conclude with a brief summary of the structure of Bosanquet's theory. Bosanquet defines punishment as the deliberate infliction of harm by a publicly authorised and recognised body onto a rational individual for her deliberate violation of publicly promulgated laws. The General Justifying Aim of punishment is the maintenance of that system of rights and obligations which 'hinders the hindrances' to the criminal's subjectively-willed attainment of her own best life. Liability under the principle of distribution is determined on a retributive basis. The court's inability to measure accurately the offender's guilt ensures, firstly that the court should not accept claims of mitigation, and secondly that it should not attempt to make the severity of the punishment proportionate to the seriousness of the crime. The severity of punishment should be determined instead, firstly by considerations of deterrence, and secondly by considerations of reform. The act of punishing the offender reaffirms to the community its adherence to the violated system of rights and obligations (and hence to the values which legitimise it). Furthermore it communicates the fact of that adherence to the criminal in such as way as might cause her to recognise her own continued reliance on that system and its values, and so repent her crime.

Obviously Bosanquet's penal theory raises a great many questions, including 'in what senses is the reassertion of social values a valuable goal?', and 'what are the implications of cultural pluralism for his communicative theory of punishment?'. Nevertheless, the present paper has at least tried to bring a little more analytical clarity and rigour to the theory than is found either in Bosanquet's own writings on punishment, or in the sparse critical literature to which it has given rise.

NOTES

1   In this paper, I use the following abbreviations to refer to Bosanquet's works: *PTS* = *The Philosophical Theory of the State*, fourth edition (London: MacMillan, 1923) (first edition was published in 1899); *GRP* = 'On the Growing Repugnance to Punishment', in his *Some Suggestions in Ethics* (London: Macmillan, 1918) (hereafter, *SSE*), 181-212.

2   Thanks go to Tony Draper, Matt Matravers for their help with references, and to Peter Nicholson and Noel O'Sullivan for their comments on the paper. Of course, they share no responsibility for my argument here.

3   Martin J Weiner, *Reconstructing the Criminal: Culture, law, and policy in England, 1830-1914* (Cambridge: CUP, 1990), 12.

4   Weiner, 1990, 12.

5   That is, *PTS*, especially chapter VIII, & *GRP*. Bosanquet's wife, Helen, records that the latter was written in 1917 (Helen Bosanquet, *Bernard Bosanquet: A short account of his life* (London: Macmillan, 1924), 138).

6   *GRP*, 181. Bosanquet argues that this distorted (therapeutic or preventative) justification of punishment has arisen from the misplaced judgement that certain abhorrent abuses were necessary features of the retributive justification of punishment (*GRP*, 181-188, 207-210).

7   'How then, and under what reservations, in the complicated conflict of the fuller and narrower self, can this dangerous drug of violence be administered, so to speak, as a counter-poison to tendencies which would otherwise give no chance to the logical will? With this difficulty in our minds, we will endeavour to determine the general principle on which force and menace should be used by the State, and a routine be mechanically maintained by it.' (*PTS*, p. 171).

8   Perceptive discussions of Bosanquet's theory of the punishment can be found in Sir
    Walter Moberly, *The Ethics of Punishment* (London: Faber and Faber, 1968). Unfortun-
    ately, although Moberly mentions Bosanquet in passing many times, he does not offer
    an integrated discussion of the theory.

9   Ted Honderich, *Punishment: The supposed justifications* (Harmondsworth: Penguin,
    1976), 46, (first edition 1969), quoting *GRP*, 190-96. Hegel's theory is set out in G.
    W. F. Hegel, *The Philosophy of Right*, translated by T. M. Knox (Oxford: OUP,
    1967), paragraphs 66 to 103.

10 Honderich, 1976, 45.

11 Alan Norrie, *Law, Ideology and Punishment: Retrieval and Critique of the Liberal Idea
    of Criminal Justice* (London: Kluwer, 1991), 110.

12 Norrie, 1991, 110. Bosanquet rejects this conflation of retribution and revenge explicitly,
    clearly and at length in *GRP*, 192-200, and 210-212. Bosanquet even goes so far as to
    state, in the Preface to *Some Suggestions in Ethics*, the fundamental question addressed
    by the essay 'On the Growing Repugnance' as, 'Is it true that retributive punishment
    is a mere survival of vindictiveness.' (*SSE*, p.v.). Clearly he answers in the negative.

13 Norrie, 1991, 110.

14 Igor Primoratz, 'The Word 'Liberty' on the Chains of Galley-Slaves: Bosanquet's Theory
    of the General Will', *History of Political Thought*, vol. XV, no. 2 (Summer 1994), 249-267.

15 Primoratz, 1994, 267.

16 '[Bosanquet] is anxious to distinguish [retribution] from vengeance, or, as he puts it,
    'an irrational vindictive impulse'.' Frederick Rosen, 'Utilitarianism and the Punishment
    of the Innocent: The Origins of a False Doctrine', *Utilitas*, vol. 9, no. 1, March 1997,
    27-28, quoting *GRP*, 192.

17 Rosen, 1997, 30. T. H. Green, 'Lectures on the Principles of Political Obligation', in
    Lectures on the Principles of Political Obligation and other writings, edited by P. Harris
    and J. Morrow (Cambridge: CUP, 1986), 138-159. F. H. Bradley, *Ethical Studies* (Oxford:
    Clarendon, 1876). F. H. Bradley, 'Some Remarks on Punishment', *International Journal
    of Ethics* (April 1894), 269-284; reprinted in his *Collected Essays* (Oxford: Clarendon,
    1969), 149-164. J. M. E. McTaggart, *Studies in Hegelian Cosomology* (Oxford: Clarendon,
    1901), chapter 5. Given their very public disputes on the issue, Rosen is clearly wrong
    to claim that Bradley and McTaggart advocated a single theory of punishment, just
    as he is wrong to conflate Green with either of them or with Bosanquet.

18 There are only a few passing references to Bosanquet's theory of punishment in William
    Sweet's important study, *Idealism and Rights: The social ontology of human rights in
    the political thought of Bernard Bosanquet* (Lanham: University Press of America,
    1997), and virtually none in Nicholson, 1990, Study VI or Alan J. M. Milne, *The Social
    Philosophy of English Idealism* (London: George Allen & Unwin, 1962).

19 *PTS*, 206. This point is repeated at *GRP*, 200-202. See Sweet, 1997, 84.

20 *GRP*, 187.

21 'Deterrence and reformation are expansions, outgrowths of its [punishment's] central
    character [as] the negation of the evil will' (*GRP*, 195).

22 *GRP*, 202.

23 *PTS*, 212.

24 *GRP*, 195.

25 H. L. A. Hart, 'Prolegomena to the Principles of Punishment', the Presidential Address
    to the Aristotelian Society (19 October 1959); reprinted in H. L. A Hart *Punishment
    and Responsibility: Essays in the Philosophy of Law* (Oxford: Clarendon, 1968), 1-27.

Hart developed these categories thirty-six years after the publication of the final (fourth) edition of *The Philosophical Theory*.

26 Émile Durkheim, *De la division du travail social: étude sur l'organisation des sociétés supérieures* (Paris, Felix Alcan, 1893). Bosanquet read this work in French (see, for example, *PTS*, 32n1 & 293n1). In this paper I will refer to the standard English edition: Emile Durkheim, *The Division of Labour in Society*, introduced by L. Coser, translated by W. D. Halls (London: MacMilan, 1984) (hereafter, *DLS*).

27 Durkheim develops his theory of social facts at greatest length in his *Les règles de la méthode sociologique*, first published in French in 1895, especially chapter two. Standard English edition is Emile Durkheim, *The Rules of Sociological Method and selected texts on sociology and its method*, translated by W. D. Halls, edited with an introduction by S. Lukes (London: Macmillan, 1982).

28 *DLS*, 52.

29 *PTS*, 205. See *GRP*, 196. For Durkheim's own statement of his position, see *DLS*, chapter 2.

30 *PTS*, 39.

31 This is one reason why Bosanquet rejects Durkheim's claim that punishment becomes 'less natural and necessary with the increase of rationality and decrease of cruelty and revenge'; when punishment sheds 'cruelty and revenge' it 'comes into its own, and reveals its fundamental significance.' (*GRP*, 192) Bosanquet ends *GRP* with this point: 'civilisation, as we said, is growing up to the import of punishment for punishment's sake, and not away from it.' (*GRP*, 212) Durkheim argues that punishment becomes less necessary to the extent that rationality becomes central to the functioning of the community, in *DLS*, chapter III *passim*.

32 *PTS*, 36.

33 *GRP*, 207. Moberly summarises this point well (Moberly, 1968, 114n1).

34 Hart, 1968, 4-5.

35 'The business of government is to promote the happiness of the society, by punishing and rewarding.' Jeremy Bentham, *Introduction to the Principles of Morals and Legislation*, edited by J. H. Burns and H. L. A. Hart (Oxford: Clarendon, 1996), Chapter VII, paragraph 1.

36 Obligations differ from duties in that duties can only be honoured when the agent acts for certain reasons (that is, because she understands the relevant imperative to be categorical), whereas an obligation can be honoured irrespective of the agent's reasons for performing the outward act required by the imperative.

37 *PTS*, 214-216.

38 Hart, 1968, 9.

39 Hart, 1968, 9.

40 As Hart notes however, 'it does not in the least follow from the admission of the latter principle of retribution in Distribution that the General Justifying Aim of punishment is Retribution though of course Retribution in General Aim entails retribution in Distribution.' (Hart, 1968, 9)

41 Hart concentrates on determining 'liability' in his 'Prolegomenon' (Hart, 1968, 11-27), and only mentions in passing the question of 'Amount' (Hart, 1968, 11).

42 Hart, 1968, 14-17.

43 Hart, 1968, 24-27.

44 Hart, 1968, 25.

45 *GRP*, 193.

46   *PTS*, 212. This point is explored at greater length in *GRP*, 203-206.

47   *PTS*, 212. Immanuel Kant, *The Metaphysics of Morals*, translated by M. Gregor (Cambridge: CUP, 1991), [Academy pagination] 331-337 *passim*. This feature of Bosanquet's position is noted by Moberly, 1968, 89n4. On the relationship between Kant and Bosanquet on punishment, see Sweet, 1997, 225-226.

48   *PTS*, 212. Kant, 1991, 332.

49   *PTS*, 212, see *ibid.*, 203-205.

50   *PTS*, 214-215. Bosanquet's response is that a crime committed under extreme condition, such as the theft of food during a famine, is a different class of crime than where conditions are not extreme, such as theft of food where food is not scarce. Consequently it should be treated differently by the legal system.

51   'The offence must not merely have moral culpability, but it must be a definite violation of explicit and social law.' (*GRP*, 207) For the clarification of this sentence, see *GRP*, 206-207.

52   Kant, 1964, 428-429.

53   *GRP*, 207.

54   *GRP*, 191.

55   Honderich, 1976, 46.

56   *GRP*, 190.

57   *GRP*, 189-190.

58   These are not Bosanquet's terms. In what follows both 'objective' and 'principal' values presuppose Raz's conception of 'ultimate values'. The latter are, 'Those things are valuable in themselves the existence of which is valuable irrespective of what else exists . . . The aspects of a good in itself which are of ultimate value are those which explain and justify the judgment that it is good in itself, and which are such that their own value need not be explained or be justified by reference to (their contribution to) other values.' (Joseph Raz, *The Morality of Freedom* (Oxford: Clarendon, 1986), 200.) An objective value is an ultimate value understood in the realist terms set out in the main body of this paper. A principal value is a value which an individual agent holds (more or less consciously) as an ultimate value (although without making any *necessary* reference to its existence or non-existence as an objective value).

59   David O. Brink, 'Moral Realism', in Robert Audi, gen. ed., *The Cambridge Dictionary of Philosophy* (Cambridge: CUP, 1995), 511a. Bosanquet is heavily influenced by Plato and Hegel here, but the precise structure of his value realism is unclear.

60   Joseph Raz, *The Morality of Freedom* (Oxford: Clarendon, 1986), 187.

61   Charles Taylor, 'Interpretation and the Sciences of Man', in his *Philosophical Papers Volume 2: Philosophy and the Human Sciences* (Cambridge: CUP, 1985), especially 36-37.

62   *GRP*, 189-191. Another reading has been suggested to me. Consider Bosanquet's reference to the pulling down of a building in the following way: the local council pulls down a building which had been erected without planning permission. There is a sense in which the building can itself be seen as 'null' – it lacked the legal status which was necessary for it to formally exist in the world. To demolish this building is, in Hegel's sense, to 'negate the negation'. The precise structure of this claim is itself a matter of intense dispute, as are its soundness and validity especially when applied to punishment. Fortunately this reading does not appear to capture Bosanquet's position, particularly when one thinks through his discussion of annulment as negating a harmful precedent, in the manner attempted in the body of the present article.

63   *GRP*, 189.

64 *GRP*, 190.

65 Bosanquet does not present the point in these terms of course.

66 The act of annulment is completed by the communicative facet of punishment, as will become clear in the next section.

67 Norrie, 1991, 111n82, citing Hasting Rashdall, *The Theory of Good and Evil, volume 1* (Oxford, Oxford University Press, 1907), 300-301n. See Rosen, 1997, 30.

68 Moberly, 1968, 99, see *ibid.*, 99-100.

69 Joel Feinberg, 'The Expressive Theory of Punishment', in A. Duff and D. Garland, *A Reader on Punishment* (Oxford: Oxford UP, 1994), 73-91. An extract from Joel Feinberg, *Doing and Deserving* (1970), 95-118.

70 Feinberg, 1994, 75, quoting Henry M. Hart, 'The Aims of the Criminal Law', *Law and Contemporary Problems*, 23 (1958), II, A, 4.

71 Feinberg, 1994, 77-78.

72 Feinberg, 1994, 78-79.

73 Feinberg, 1994, 79.

74 Feinberg, 1994, 79-80.

75 '. . . we reserve . . . the term "reprobation" for the stern judgment of disapproval' (Feinberg, 1994, 77).

76 *GRP*, 193.

77 *PTS*, 208.

78 Primoratz, 1994, 262-263.

79 *PTS*, 210.

80 Norrie, 1991, 109.

81 *PTS*, 208.

82 Notice (contra Norrie, 1991, 109) that Bosanquet does not 'concede' that the strength of retributivism lies in 'its definite idea of the offender'; he simply affirms it.

83 Kant, 1964, 397-401. Sweet, 1997, 34n1.

84 It is difficult to know what reasons anyone could have for supporting the institution of punishment if they did not see something positive in it.

85 *GRP*, 211.

86 *PTS*, xxxii, see *ibid.*, xxxi-xxxii.

87 For example, by not paying the required taxes, an agent undermines the effectiveness of the police force and thereby makes her property and life less secure.

88 *PTS*, 207.

89 *PTS*, . 206. 'Men' in the sense of particular agents, I take it.

90 *PTS*, 209. See Sweet's brief discussion of this passage (Sweet, 1997, 167).

91 R. A. Duff, *Trials and Punishments* (Cambridge: CUP, 1986), especially chapter 9. Andrew von Hirsch, *Censure and Sanctions* (Oxford: OUP, 1993). R. A. Duff, 'Penal Communications', *Crime and Justice: A Review of Research*, (1996) 20, 1-97. R. A. Duff, 'Punishment, Communication, and Community', in Matt Matravers, ed., *Punishment and Political Theory* (Oxford: Hart, 1999), 48-68 and 'Response to von Hirsch, in Matravers, ed., 1999, 83-87. Andrew von Hirsch, 'Punishment, Penance, and the State: A Reply to Duff', in Matravers, ed., 1999, 69-82. There are other very interesting discussions of the communicative theory in Matravers, ed., 1999: in particular see the contributions by Ivison, Matravers and Baldwin. The similarities between contemporary discussions and those of Bosanquet is probably not due to any direct influence of the latter on the former. In fact it probably results from there being a shared debt to Hegel (Duff, 1986, 262-266).

92 Duff, 1986, 238.
93 Von Hirsch, 1999, 69. Hegel made a similar point (especially Hegel, 1967, paragraph 99 (Addition); also *ibid.*, paragraphs 93, 100 (Remark)), as did Green in the *Principles* (Green, 1986, 144-145, 153-154).
94 Duff continues in parenthesis: 'as well as by 'mediation' schemes whose aim is to bring the offender to recognise the nature and implications of what she has done, and thus to make material or symbolic reparation for it' (Duff, 1999, 53).
95 *PTS*, 212-216.
96 *PTS*, 216.
97 *GRP*, 193, emphasis added.
98 Notice in particular *GRP*, 181-188, 207-210.
99 *GRP*, 210.
100 *PTS*, 213.
101 It is misnamed because 'mediation' implies that the victim should reach a compromise with the criminal. In fact it is only the criminal who should compromise, by recognising and publicly acknowledging the wrongness of her crime.
102 *PTS*, 206.
103 *PTS*, 210, as quoted at Norrie, 1991, 109.
104 *PTS*, 211.
105 *PTS*, 197.

Review

David Boucher, James Connelly and Tariq Modood (eds.), *Philosophy, History and Civilization: Interdisciplinary Perspectives on R. G. Collingwood.* Cardiff: University of Wales Press, 1995. xviii + 388 pp. ISBN 0-7083-1308-6 (hbk).

By Stamatoula Panagakou, York University.

This book is invaluable reading to all students, academics and scholars who are interested in the philosophy of R. G. Collingwood and in British Philosophical Idealism. David Boucher, Margot Browning, James Connelly, T. J. Diffey, Jan van der Dussen, B. A. Haddock, H. S. Harris, Ian Hodder, the late Donald M. MacKinnon, Rex Martin, the late A. J. M. Milne, Tariq Modood, Adrian Oldfield, Rik Peters and Leon Pompa discuss and reassess the entire range of Collingwood's engagement with philosophy. The authors unravel Collingwood's complex arguments and ideas, focus on controversial issues, trace influences and intellectual affinities, elaborate new analyses and interpretations, and demonstrate the significance and originality of his theorising. *Philosophy, History and Civilization* offers new insights into the work of one of the most important British Idealists, and provides a sound basis for further research and explorations.

In 'The Life, Times and Legacy of R. G. Collingwood' Boucher introduces thematically the chapters in *Philosophy, History and Civilization* and sketches an informative outline of Collingwood's life and intellectual development, of his intellectual relations with other philosophers, and of the resonance of his ideas. Collingwood was influenced by the Italian Idealists Croce, Gentile and de Ruggiero. His philosophy has some affinities with the work of A. J. Ayer, L. Wittgenstein, J. L. Austin and G. Ryle.

M. Oakeshott, J. Levenson, A. Linklater and M. J. R. Healy have been inspired by Collingwood's philosophical essays. Collingwood's contributions to the history of ideas and hermeneutics have been acknowledged by Greenleaf, Pocock, Dunn, Skinner, Gadamer, Bultmann, Pannenberg, Lonergan and Ricoeur. His theory of absolute presuppositions anticipated questions later asked by Feyerabend, Kuhn and Hanson. Collingwood's extensive influence on many fields of study continues to grow with the availability of his unpublished manuscripts.

'Collingwood and the Idea of Philosophy' by Modood examines Collingwood's endeavour to develop a philosophical system in accordance with the idea of philosophy as the principle of cultural unity. Collingwood was a philosopher aspiring to grand theory: he was interested in elaborating a systematic framework for evaluating all the aspects of human activity. In Collingwood's view, philosophy has the task of creating a new cultural unity appropriate to the modern world. Philosophy revolves around experience and seeks to situate the part within a wider whole in order to achieve comprehensive explanation. Philosophical reasoning is non-axiomatic and open to ceaseless critical reflection. In Collingwood's philosophical scale of forms, each species of a philosophical genus is a stage in conceptual development. To understand the significance of a species is to comprehend it as one in a logically interrelated and progressive series. According to Modood, this is a dialectical series.

Diffey argues in his 'Aesthetics and Philosophical Method' that there is an indispensable connection between Collingwood's aesthetics and his method because he had his own distinctive view of philosophy. Collingwood's philosophy of art must be seen as a development of the philosophical tradition from Descartes to Kant. *The Principles of Art* is a very significant contribution to aesthetics: 'an unusual fusion of cultural criticism and the philosophy of mind' (p. 63). Collingwood is concerned with the question 'why is art important to us?' and he proceeds to elaborate a theory about what makes emotion expressed in art truthful. Contrary to the 'institutionalists' who follow the Wittgensteinians and tell us how the term 'art' is used, Collingwood explains what art properly is and which are the improper uses of the term. He thus constructs an account of art that is consistent with the critical and reflective nature of philosophy and propounds a criteriological aesthetic.

MacKinnon, in 'Faith and Reason in the Philosophy of Religion', argues that Collingwood's article 'Reason is Faith Cultivating Itself' is one of his most valuable contributions to the philosophy of religion. The article was published in the *Hibbert Journal* for 1927. In his earlier writing, Collingwood identified the world of faith with the world of the experience of life as it is lived. Collingwood follows Anselm's project of relating faith and logic and adheres to 'the Anselmian rubric *fides quaerens intellectum*' (p. 88). Echoes of the *Hibbert Journal* article are found in Collingwood's later work. It is difficult, however, to crystallise 'an easily definable philosophy of religion' (p. 88) from Collingwood's writings.

Connelly in 'Art Thou the Man: Croce, Gentile or de Ruggiero?' argues that Guido de Ruggiero was the key figure for Collingwood. Collingwood's interest in historical philosophy distanced him from both the Realists and the Idealists who were not historically-minded. He was impressed by the historical awareness exhibited by his contemporary Italian philosophy. Collingwood was indebted to Croce, but their relationship was not one of equals. Croce was the philosopher that Collingwood admired, respected, and rebelled against. His relationship with Gentile was 'complicated by politics' (p. 103). Collingwood denounced Gentile because he was a fascist, yet, he continued to draw silently on his doctrines. Collingwood's relationship with de Ruggiero was characterised by free exchange of ideas, reciprocity, openness and willingness to discuss on equal terms.

Harris's 'Croce and Gentile in Collingwood's *New Leviathan*' focuses on the first part of *The New Leviathan* in which Collingwood expounds his theory of 'Man' and offers an account of the intellectual influences, especially the Italian influences, that can be identified. The conceptual means by which Collingwood establishes a direct link between his work and that of the materialist Hobbes is provided by the idealist Gentile. Collingwood regarded feeling as the object of consciousness and elaborated his theory in *The Principles of Art* and *The New Leviathan* in order to prove the inadequacies of the Italian Idealists. Unlike Croce and Gentile, Collingwood was critically appreciative of Freud and of his followers. His theory of utility was not influenced by the dichotomous approach of the two Italians. Collingwood's theory of right is inspired by Bradley, while his theory of duty is Croccan. Collingwood 'naturalized' the philosophy of Croce and Gentile and studied the latest introspective psychology:

by doing so, 'he became the genuinely original philosopher of mind that he really is' (p. 127).

In 'Vico, Collingwood and the Character of a Historical Philosophy' Haddock claims that Vico 'can be seen to have an abiding presence throughout Collingwood's career' (p. 131) and examines points of both convergence and divergence in their respective theories. Between Collingwood and Vico there is a fundamental methodological divide. Collingwood distinguishes between critical and speculative philosophy of history; for Vico, however, this distinction could not arise. Both Collingwood and Vico rejected the view of philosophy as a self-contained discipline that is unrelated to other modes of experience. Vico, Croce and Collingwood attributed an epistemological significance to imagination. Vico and Collingwood were concerned with the historical dimension in philosophy. Collingwood endorsed 'an essentially Vichian conception of history as the key to a science of human conduct' (p. 149).

The subject of Peters's 'Croce, Gentile and Collingwood on the Relation between History and Philosophy' is Collingwood's *rapprochement* between philosophy and history in the light of the debate between Croce and Gentile on the same topic. Croce conceives of history as the beginning and end of all thinking – philosophy is an aspect of history. Gentile claims that philosophy is the beginning and end of all thinking – history is only an aspect of philosophy. Peters argues that Collingwood was helped by Croce's theory of history considered as individual judgement and by Gentile's epistemological view of the historian creating history by his act of thinking. However, both Croce's dialectic of distincts and Gentile's version of 'the subjective, monoperspectival eternal act which was characteristic of fascist egocentrism' (p. 163) left Collingwood dissatisfied.

Pompa's 'Collingwood's Theory of Historical Knowledge' is a critical assessment of Collingwood's account of the way in which we acquire historical knowledge. Pompa argues that Collingwood developed a largely correct, yet, incomplete account of historical knowledge because he overlooked the phenomenon of historical consciousness. Collingwood sees historians as rational inquirers who take nothing for granted, accept no authorities, and base solely their conclusions on inferential methods. Historians, however, are historical products and they do not theorise on history from a vantage-point outside history. Historians possess a historical consciousness which formulates a body of inherited knowledge. Collingwood, in his endeavour to preserve the thesis of historical autonomy, overlooked the point that historical knowledge is based on cultural inheritance, i.e., on a cluster of known historical facts that cultures acquire historically, rather than on rational inference. The thesis of historical autonomy does not mean the absolute absence of fixed points.

In 'Metaphysics and History in Collingwood's Thought' Oldfield argues that the theory of absolute presuppositions does not inhibit the possibility of historical knowledge. He claims that Collingwood was an epistemological pluralist and refutes Toulmin's thesis that he was an epistemological relativist. Oldfield argues that the re-enactment of thought is the characteristic feature of historical knowledge. The object of historical knowledge is thought because only thought can be re-enacted. Historical knowledge is acquired by inferential argument: re-enactment is the conclusion of an inferential argument. The dialectical interpretation of absolute presuppositions solves the problem of historical knowledge. Martin and Toulmin discern a radical discontinuity between different constellations of absolute presuppositions that would inhibit the possibility of historical knowledge. Oldfield's argument is an objection to this thesis.

In 'Collingwood's Claim that Metaphysics is a Historical Discipline' Martin contends that Collingwood did not intend to provide the re-enactment account of metaphysics, and that the key to his claim that metaphysics is a historical discipline is his views on processes. Absolute presuppositions are not to be explained by re-enactment because the latter refers to the explanation and understanding of actions. Absolute presuppositions stand in a relationship of progressive improvement within a process of development. Contrary to Knox's and Donagan's view that there is a doctrinal break between Collingwood's two essays on metaphysics, Martin discerns an unbroken continuity. The idea that absolute presuppositions are wholly involved in historical processes of development is integrated with the modified scale-of-forms pattern of analysis.

Van der Dussen's 'Collingwood on the Ideas of Process, Progress and Civilization' offers a conceptual clarification of the aforementioned notions in Collingwood's philosophy. Collingwood distinguishes clearly between natural and historical processes. A natural process is characterised by a mere time-sequence. A historical process is characterised by the encapsulation of the past in the present. Van der Dussen identifies four positions in Collingwood's views on the concept of progress. He rejects the objective nature of historical progress. He argues that progress must be understood in the context of historical periods and that the historian must see the past as a participant in the historical process. He claims that the concept of progress is necessary as a guiding principle. In Collingwood's philosophy of history, the process of civilisation has two aspects: the aspect of the inheritance from the past and the aspect of human will. Human will is the basis for progress in civilisation.

In 'The Place of Education in Civilization', Boucher asserts that Collingwood believed education to play a fundamental role in the development of civilisation and the formation of character. To understand his thoughts on education one needs to adopt a holistic approach. The purpose of education is the attainment of cognitive competence and the realisation of the ideal of civility. The content of education must provide an understanding of all forms of experience. Collingwood's account of the manner of education has two features: distrusting the specialist and entrusting parents with the education of their children. Boucher criticises Collingwood's blind optimism, his idyllic view of a rural England, and his inability to see England in terms of social classes. He acknowledges, however, that Collingwood 'displayed genuine insights in warning of the dangers of a technocratic and utilitarian civilization' (p. 295).

Milne's 'Civilization and the Open Society: Collingwood and Popper' is a comparative critical assessment of *The New Leviathan* and *The Open Society and Its Enemies*. Milne's main thesis is that Collingwood and Popper, despite their different approaches, shared the same concern for the survival of modern European civilisation. Popper's critical rationalism makes a society open and Collingwood's dialectical attitude accounts for a civilised society. Milne reached the following conclusions. None of the two philosophers dealt satisfactorily with the question of morality. Collingwood offers no account of government, and Popper, although he refers to the modern European democratic state, did not develop a systematic narrative of its procedures. Popper failed to distinguish between Nazism's irrationalism and Marxism's defective rationalism and, in addition, he did not appreciate the difference between scientific and historical understanding. Collingwood acknowledges the contribution of past philosophers. In sum, although both approaches are complementary, Collingwood's is the more fruitful.

In 'A Baconian Revolution: Collingwood and Romano-British Studies', Browning argues that Collingwood developed a theory of scientific revolutions in the Baconian tradition and became its proponent in Romano-British studies. Collingwood's discussion of the problem of the Roman Wall represents his interdisciplinary interpretation of science, history and archaeology. Collingwood's philosophy of history is Idealist in its orientation, but it has an empiricist dimension deriving from its historical contextualisation. Collingwood's theory of scientific revolutions has philosophical, historical and archaeological elements and combines characteristics of the revolutionary model, the evolutionary model and the growth model for the history of science. Collingwood's theory of scientific revolutions emphasises the similarities between scientific history and natural science, yet, his codification of Baconian principles for historical method distinguishes between knowledge of nature and knowledge of humanity.

Hodder's 'Of Mice and Men: Collingwood and the Development of Archaeological Thought' offers an engaging discussion of the renewed interest in Collingwood's work. Hodder identifies five ways in which Collingwood's approach is relevant to theoretical debate in contemporary archaeology. These five aspects are: (a) the opposition between the historical and natural sciences; (b) the theory of action; (c) the use of generalisations; (d) the validation of particular historical interpretations; and (e) the political nature of archaeological knowledge. According to Hodder, Collingwood did not have a thoroughly critical perspective regarding his methodology, and he did not consider such components as self, power and ideology. Contemporary archaeology has much to learn from both the failures and successes of Collingwood's theoretical and methodological system.

Boucher, Connelly and Modood set themselves a difficult task and achieved its fruitful completion. Sixteen critical essays written by leading Collingwood scholars provide the reader with fascinating analyses of all the aspects of Collingwood's philosophy and prove the everlasting freshness and unique originality of his theorising. *Philosophy, History and Civilization: Interdisciplinary Perspectives on R. G. Collingwood* is a lively, thought-provoking and intellectually demanding book that deserves to be widely read and discussed.

LIFE MEMBERS OF THE COLLINGWOOD SOCIETY

Dr Michael Beaney, David Blatchford, Professor David Boucher, Professor George Boyce, Dr Jonathan Bradbury, Professor R. Bradley, Lord Bragg, Rt. Hon. Lord Callaghan, Dr O. Caraiani, Anna Castriota, Mrs Mary Clapinson, Mr Bruce Coffin, Professor Janet Coleman, Rev. Jeremy Collingwood, Professor Conal Condren, Dr James Connelly, Dr Susan Daniel, Professor William Debbins, Mr Robin Denniston, Professor William Dray, Professor John Dunn, Professor David Eastwood, Dr Albert Fell, Dr Joe Femia, Mr Peter Foden, Rt. Hon. Michael Foot, Dr Elizabeth Frazer, Professor Frank Gilliard, Miss Janet Gnosspelius, Professor Leon Goldstein, David A. Griffiths, Dr Margit Hurup Grove, Professor Knud Haakonssen, Dr Bruce Haddock, Professor H. S. Harris, Dr Stein Helgeby, Professor Michael Hinz, Mr Sinclair Hood, John Horton, Dr John Hospers, Dr Marnie Hughes-Warrington, Sue Irving, Professor Wendy James, Professor Jeremy Jennings, Dr Douglas Johnson, Dr Peter Johnson, Susie Johnston, Professor William Johnston, Dr Norman Jones, Dr Maurice Keens-Soper, Professor Donald Kelley, Dr Paul Kelly, Professor Kenneth Ketner, Professor Michael Krausz, Julian Lethbridge, Peter Lewis, George Livadas, Dr Florin Lobont, Professor Alasdair MacIntyre, Dr Maria Markoczy, Professor Rex Martin, Neville Masterman, Wayne Mastin, Donald Matthews, Dr C. Behan McCullagh, Dr Graham McFee, Ken McIntyre, Hugh McLean, Iain Miller, Professor Kenneth Minogue, Dr Ivan Molloy, Timothy Morgan, Professor Myra Moss, Richard Murphy, Professor Terry Nardin, Professor Jay Newman, Peter Nicholson, Dr Francis O'Gorman, Dr Robert Orr, Elizabeth Pakis, Professor Carole Pateman, Roy Pateman, Dr Zbigniew Pelczynski, Dr Rik Peters, Lord Professor Raymond Plant, Professor Clementina Gily Reda, Dr Angela Requate, Dr Dwaine Richins, William Rieckmann, Dr Peri Roberts, Professor Lionel Rubinoff, Professor Alan Ryan, Mrs Brigit Sanders, Herman Simissen, Dr Grace Simpson, Professor Quentin Skinner, Mrs Teresa Smith, Robert Stevens, Guy Stock, Peter Strong, Dr Hidemi Suganami, Sherwood Sugden, Dr Peter Sutch, Professor Donald S. Taylor, Professor Richard Taylor, Leo Ten Hag, Rt. Hon. The Baroness Thatcher, Dr Julian Thomas, Dr Martyn P. Thompson, Professor Jan van der Dussen, Naomi van Loo, Professor Guido Vanheeswijck, Professor Donald Verene, Professor Andrew Vincent, Dr Kallistes Ware, Dr Lawrence Wilde, Professor Howard Williams, Andrew F. Wilson, Dr Adrian Wilson, Dr Ian Winchester, Professor David Wood, Andrew Wright, Dr Elizabeth Wright.

Journal of Political Ideologies

EDITOR

Michael Freeden, *Mansfield College, Oxford, UK*

Supported by Associate Editors and an International Editorial Board

The *Journal of Political Ideologies* is dedicated to the analysis of political ideology both in its theoretical and conceptual aspects, and with reference to the nature and roles of concrete ideological manifestations.

The journal promotes research into political ideologies, which are indispensable to the understanding of political thought within social, temporal and spatial contexts. It emphasizes both the general phenomenon of ideologies and their particular instances. In parallel, it underlines that political action, processes and institutions are endowed with ideological import and shaped to a considerable extent by political ideologies.

This journal is also available online.
Please connect to http://www.tandf.co.uk/online.html for further information.

SUBSCRIPTION RATES

2001 – Volume 6 (3 issues)
Print ISSN 1356-9317
Online ISSN 1469-9613
Institutional rate: US$249; £150 (includes free online access)
Personal rate: US$59; £37 (print only)

- -

ORDER FORM

cjpi

PLEASE COMPLETE IN BLOCK CAPITALS AND RETURN TO THE ADDRESS BELOW

Please invoice me at the ☐ **institutional rate** ☐ **personal rate**

☐ Please send me a sample copy

Name _____

Address _____

_____

_____

E-mail _____

Please contact Customer Services at either:

Taylor & Francis Ltd, Rankine Road, Basingstoke, Hants RG24 8PR, UK
Tel: +44 (0)1256 813002 **Fax:** +44 (0)1256 330245 **E-mail:** enquiry@tandf.co.uk **www:** http://www.tandf.co.uk

Taylor & Francis Inc, 325 Chestnut Street, 8th Floor, Philadelphia, PA 19106, USA
Fax: +1 215 625 2940 **E-mail:** info@taylorandfrancis.com **www:** http://www.taylorandfrancis.com

R. G. COLLINGWOOD NEW MILLENNIUM CONFERENCE

St. Catherine's College, Oxford
4-6 July, 2001

Speakers: Rex Martin, David Boucher, Peter Skagestad, Tim Lord, Richard Allen, Michael Beaney, Tim Rosser, Gary Browning, Angela Requate, Andrew Wright, Ian Winchester, Josie D'Oro, David Holt and Heikki Saari.

Collingwood & British Idealism Studies
Formerly Collingwood Studies
Back Issues now available at £12-00 per volume.

Subscriptions
Membership 1 Year £12-00 individuals: Libraries £20-00: Students £6-00
SPECIAL OFFER: 5 YEAR MEMBERSHIP £60
Plus a free copy of, *The Social and Political Thought of R. G. Collingwood* by David Boucher (RRP £45); or, *A Radical Hegelian: the Social and Political Thought of Henry Jones* by David Boucher and Andrew Vincent (RRP £45); or, Peter Johnson, *R. G. Collingwood's Correspondence* (RRP £20)

R. G. Collingwood's Correspondence
An Illustrated Guide
Peter Johnson
Southampton University

Johnson identifies, specifies the location and gives an account of every item of Collingwood's correspondence currently known, including the extensive holdings in the Clarendon Press Archive. This is an invaluable aid to research in all aspects of Collingwood's thought. With 7 illustrations -- photographs of and taken by Collingwood, drawings by Collingwood and facsimile letter.
ISBN 0 952439 3 6 Hardback
Price £20-00 (inc. postage and packing)

For details of the Conference, membership and book orders please contact Suzi Williams, The Collingwood and British Idealism Centre, School of European Studies, PO Box 908, Cardiff CF10 3YQ, UK. FAX 44 (0) 29 2087 4946. E-mail WilliamsSE6@cardiff.ac.uk or visit our website at :

http://www.cf.ac.uk/euros/Collingwood/Collingwood.html

HISTORY OF POLITICAL THOUGHT

Voted one of the best international political
science journals in *Political Studies* review[†]

History of Political Thought is a quarterly journal, launched in 1980, and devoted
exclusively to the historical study of political ideas and associated methodological
problems. All articles are refereed. ISSN 0143-781 x. Vol. XX, 1999 (4 issues, inc.
post): Libraries: $126; Individuals: $59; Students: $45 (UK inland: £60/£30/£25).

Polis

The Journal of the Society for the Study of
Greek Political Thought

Since 1978, *Polis* has published refereed articles and reviews on ancient Greek political thought by classicists, philosophers, historians & political scientists. V.16,
1999, annual, ISSN 0412-257 x. Libraries: $31.50; Individuals: $21 (UK: £15/£12).

Orders/enquiries: Imprint Academic, PO Box 1, Thorverton, EX5 5YX, UK.

Phone/Fax: +44 1392 841600   sandra@imprint.co.uk   http://www.imprint.co.uk

Name . . . . Address . . . .

. . . .

FREE Illustrated Hobbes special issue with every new *HPT* subscription

☐ Please send brochure/sample copy ☐ *History of Political Thought* ☐ *Polis*
☐ Cheque, pay 'Imprint Academic' ☐ Please bill me ☐ Charge Visa/MC/Amex

No. . . . . Exp . . . . Signed . . . .

† Norris & Crewe, 'The Reputation of political science journals', *Political Studies*, XLI, pp. 5-23.